Good Old Days® Remembers

Mother's Favorite Verses™

Edited by Ken and Janice Tate

HOUSE of
WHITE
BIRCHES
PUBLISHERS
SINCE 1947

Good Old Days® Remembers Mother's Favorite Verses

Editors: Ken and Janice Tate
Associate Editor: Barb Sprunger
Copy Editors: Läna Schurb, Mary Nowak

Production Coordinator: Brenda Gallmeyer
Graphic Arts Supervisor: Ronda Bechinski
Design/Production Artist: Erin Augsburger
Cover Design: Jessi Butler
Traffic Coordinator: Sandra Beres
Production Assistants: Janet Bowers, Marj Morgan, Chad Tate
Photography: Tammy Christian, Jeff Chilcote, Justin P. Wiard
Photography Assistant: Linda Quinlan
Photography Stylist: Arlou Wittwer

Publishers: Carl H. Muselman, Arthur K. Muselman
Chief Executive Officer: John Robinson
Marketing Director: Scott Moss
Product Development Director: Vivian Rothe
Publishing Services Manager: Brenda Wendling

Customer Service: (800) 829-5865
Printed in the United States of America
First Printing: 2001
Library of Congress Number: 00-109008
ISBN: 1-882138-67-8

Every effort has been made to ensure the accuracy of the material in this book. However,
the publisher is not responsible for research errors or typographical mistakes in this publication.

We would like to thank the following for the art prints used in this book:
Apple Creek Publishing: *Home Sweet Home* by Kim Norlien, pages 108 and 109. For information on art prints,
contact Apple Creek Publishing, Hiawatha, IA 52233, (800) 662-1707.

Mill Pond Press: *Bedtime Story* by Jim Daly, front cover; *Storybook Dreams* by Jim Daly, pages 4 and 5; *Spring Fever* by Jim Daly,
pages 8 and 9; *The Confrontation* by Jim Daly, page 14; *Swapping Fish Stories* by Jim Daly, page 52; *Homeward Bound*
by Peter Ellenshaw, pages 60 and 61; *Safe Passage* by Luke Buck, pages 140 and 141; and *Path at Giverny* by Peter Ellenshaw,
page 155. For information on art prints, contact Mill Pond Press, Venice, FL 34292, (800) 535-0331.

Wild Wings Inc.: *Harvest Time* by Sam Timm, pages 36 and 37; and *Peeping Toms* by Lee Kromschroeder, page 48.
For information on art prints, contact Wild Wings Inc., Lake City, MN 55041, (800) 445-4833.

Dear Friends of the Good Old Days,

Good Old Days magazine began publication in the early 1960s with one mission in mind. It was billed as "the magazine that remembers the best," and for nearly four decades has helped keep the Good Old Days alive.

My dear wife Janice and I have been with the magazine nearly a third of its life; 12 years at the time of this writing. I was an avid reader of the magazine beginning in its early years, and Janice and I were excited when the publishers asked us to take over the editorial reins.

One of the chief reasons I was so drawn to the magazine was the readership of the magazines and that readership's willingness to help others. That was best demonstrated by a column, "Wanteds," that has been an important part of the magazine since its beginning.

Probably the most requested items in the Wanteds have been the words to poetry and songs. In most cases, the verse was something mothers and fathers read or sang. On the other hand, perhaps they were among those memorized for school recitations or programs. If songs, they may have been played on an old Victrola or over the radio.

Janice and I began to compile a list of the most-requested poems and songs from the Wanteds. We began referring to them as "Mother's Favorite Verses"—and that ultimately was the genesis of this book.

We have consulted as many sources as possible to confirm the accuracy of the words to these verses. That being said, slightly different wording is the nature of many folk poems and songs. Where more than one set of words showed up in our research, we have tried to use the set that is more popularly known. I'm sure that readers of this volume will remember variations on these popular poems and songs.

We have included indexes at the end of the book—for title, author (if known), first line and last line. We hope these will help you locate specific poems or songs.

What was important to Janice and me was that these lines, so dear to so many people, be preserved. Thanks go to the thousands of readers who have requested these verses—and to those who answered the Wanteds and sent hundreds of verses and pieces of music to the magazine to share with other readers.

I know these lines will remind you of days snuggled in your mother's lap, learning early the love of literature. These poems and songs would be among my own mother's picks—I know because she spent hundreds of hours reading and singing them to me in my youth. Likewise, I hope they are among your Mother's Favorite Verses.

Ken Tate

Contents

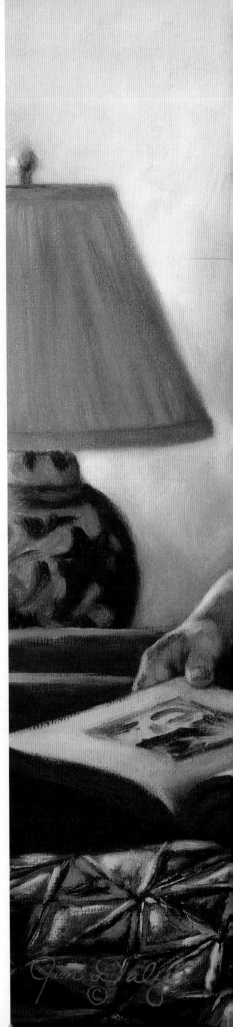

In Our Youth

Chapter One

*E*very time I think of poetry from the Good Old Days, I think of the first time I had to memorize verse for some school function. I don't remember now if it was some gathering of county officials, or just an assembly of a small school's parents, but my teacher wanted me to recite "The Wind and the Leaves" by George Cooper.

I agonized over those 20 lines more than I did any part in a Christmas play, more than the Preamble to the Constitution, more than the Gettysburg Address. The fact is, I thought at the time the poem was a "sissy" verse and that no self-respecting man would be caught dead reciting it.

In later years I came to have a greater appreciation for the poetry I was forced to memorize as a boy. As you read through the verse selected for this chapter, you will be reminded of the many times our mothers, teachers and other mentors impressed us with these lines we learned in our youth.

—*Ken Tate*

The Wind and the Leaves

By George Cooper

"Come, little Leaves," said the Wind one day,
"Come over the meadows with me and play;
Put on your dresses of red and gold,
For summer is gone and the days grow cold."

Soon as the Leaves heard the Wind's loud call,
Down they came fluttering, one and all;
Over the brown fields they danced and flew,
Singing the sweet little song they knew:
"Cricket, good-bye, we've been friends so long;
Little Brook, sing us your farewell song;
Say you are sorry to see us go;
Ah, you will miss us, right well we know.
Dear little lambs in your fleecy fold,
Mother will keep you from harm and cold;
Fondly we watched you in vale and glade,

Say, will you dream of our loving shade?"
Dancing and whirling, the little Leaves went,
Winter had called them, and they were content:
Soon, fast asleep in their earthy beds,
The snow laid a coverlid over their heads.

Rock Me to Sleep

By Elizabeth Akers Allen

Backward, turn backward, O Time, in your flight,
Make me a child again just for to-night!
Mother, come back from the echoless shore,
Take me again to your heart as of yore;
Kiss from my forehead the furrows of care,
Smooth the few silver threads out of my hair;
Over my slumbers your loving watch keep;—
Rock me to sleep, Mother—rock me to sleep!

Backward, flow backward, O tide of the years!
I am so weary of toil and of tears—
Toil without recompense, tears all in vain—
Take them, and give me my childhood again!
I have grown weary of dust and decay—
Weary of flinging my soul-wealth away;
Weary of sowing for others to reap;—
Rock me to sleep, Mother—rock me to sleep!

Tired of the hollow, the base, the untrue,
Mother, O Mother, my heart calls for you!
Many a summer the grass has grown green,
Blossomed and faded, our faces between:
Yet, with strong yearning and passionate pain,
Long I to-night for your presence again.
Come from the silence so long and so deep;—
Rock me to sleep, Mother—rock me to sleep!

Over my heart, in the days that are flown,
No love like mother-love ever has shone;
No other worship abides and endures—
Faithful, unselfish, and patient like yours:
None like a mother can charm away pain
From the sick soul and the world-weary brain.
Slumber's soft calms o'er my heavy lids creep;—
Rock me to sleep, Mother—rock me to sleep!

Come, let your brown hair, just lighted with gold,
Fall on your shoulders again as of old;
Let it drop over my forehead to-night,
Shading my faint eyes away from the light;
For with its sunny-edged shadows once more
Haply will throng the sweet visions of yore;
Lovingly, softly, its bright billows sweep;—
Rock me to sleep, Mother—rock me to sleep!

Mother, dear Mother, the years have been long
Since I last listened your lullaby song;
Sing, then, and unto my soul it shall seem
Womanhood's years have been only a dream.
Clasped to your heart in a loving embrace,
With your light lashes just sweeping my face,
Never hereafter to wake or to weep;—
Rock me to sleep, Mother—rock me to sleep!

In School-Days

By John Greenleaf Whittier

Still sits the school-house by the road,
A ragged beggar sunning;
Around it still the sumachs grow,
And blackberry vines are running.

Within, the master's desk is seen,
Deep scarred by raps official;
The warping floor, the battered seats,
The jack-knife's carved initial;

The charcoal frescoes on its wall;
Its door's worn sill, betraying
The feet that, creeping slow to school,
Went storming out to playing!

Long years ago a winter sun
Shone over it at setting;
Lit up its western window-panes,
And low eaves' icy fretting.

It touched the tangled golden curls
And brown eyes full of grieving,
Of one who still her steps delayed
When all the school were leaving.

For near her stood the little boy
Her childish favour singled:
His cap pulled low upon a face
Where pride and shame were mingled.

Pushing with restless feet the snow
To right and left, he lingered—
As restlessly her tiny hands
The blue-checked apron fingered.

He saw her lift her eyes; he felt
The soft hand's light caressing,
And heard the tremble of her voice,
As if a fault confessing.

"I'm sorry that I spelt the word:
I hate to go above you,
Because" —the brown eyes lower fell—
"Because, you see, I love you!"

Still memory to a grey-haired man
That sweet child-face is showing.
Dear girl! the grasses on her grave
Have forty years been growing.

He lives to learn, in life's hard school,
How few who pass above him
Lament their triumph and his loss,
Like her,—because they love him.

Johnny's History Lesson

By Nixon Waterman

I think, of all the things at school
A boy has got to do,
That studyin' hist'ry, as a rule,
Is worst of all, don't you?
Of dates there are an awful sight,
An' tho' I study day an' night,
There's only one I've got just right—
　　That's 1492.

Columbus crossed the Delaware
　　In 1492;
We whipped the British, fair an' square,
　　In 1492,
At Concord an' at Lexington
We kept the redcoats on the run
While the band played, "Johnny, get your gun,"
　　In 1492.

Pat Henry, with his dyin' breath—
　　In 1492—
Said, "Give me liberty or death"
　　In 1492.
An' Barbara Frietchie, so 'tis said,
Cried: "Shoot, if you must, this old, gray head;
But I'd rather it be your own instead!"
　　In 1492.

The Pilgrims came to Plymouth Rock
　　In 1492.
An' the Indians standin' on the dock
Asked: "What are you goin' to do?"
An' they said: "We seek your harbor drear
That our children's children's children dear,
May boast that their forefathers landed here,
　　In 1492."

Miss Pocahontas saved the life,
　　In 1492,
Of John Smith, an' became his wife
　　In 1492.
An' the Smith tribe started then an' there,
An' now, there are John Smiths everywhere,
But they didn't have any Smiths to spare
　　In 1492.

Kentucky was settled by Daniel Boone
　　In 1492,
An' I think the cow jumped over the moon,
　　In 1492.
Ben Franklin flew his kite so high
He drew the lightnin' from the sky,
An' Washington couldn't tell a lie
　　In 1492.

I Go to School Now
Author Unknown

I go to school now every day,
I know my letters all;
I used to think that X was K
But that's when I was small.

My teacher wears a bunch of curls
That isn't like her braid;
My brother Jack says,
"Switches are a schoolmarm's
    badge of trade."

I gotta seat all by myself
Just like a little chair;
One side of me is Flora Smith,
The other Sue Sinclair.

There are some boys go to our school,
I wish they didn't though;
They're worser than the worstest girl,
The teacher says it's so.

Tom Baker pulled Nell Avery's hair,
And Archibald Magee

Poured a whole cup of water
Down on Flora Smith and me.

My kitty followed me to school
Last Wednesday afternoon;
I didn't have time to take her home;
The bell would ring so soon.

I put her slyly in my desk,
The teacher didn't see,
And thought she'd sleep 'till school
    was out
And then go home with me.

But when my class was called to read,
She got me in disgrace;
She just climbed out on top the desk,
Sat down and washed her face.

The teacher made me put her out;
I cried like anything,
She got home safe before me, though,
Good-bye, I'm going to swing.

Twenty Froggies
By George Cooper

Twenty froggies went to school
Down beside a rushy pool;
Twenty little coats of green,
Twenty vests all white and clean.

"We must be in time," said they.
"First we study, then we play;
That is how we keep the rule,
When we froggies go to school."

Master Bull-Frog, grave and stern,
Called his classes in their turn;
Taught them how to nobly strive,
Likewise how to leap and dive.

From his seat upon the log,
Taught them how to say, "Ker-chog!"
Likewise how to dodge the blows
From the stick which bad boys throw.

Twenty froggies grew up fast;
Big frogs they became at last.
Not one dunce among the lot,
Not one lesson they forgot.

Polished in a high degree,
As a froggie ought to be,
Now they sit on other logs,
Teaching other little frogs.

Childhood's Prayer

By Newton Ottis

As now I lay me down to sleep,
May angel guards around
me keep,
Through all the silent hours
of night,
Their watch and ward till
morning light.
Dim evening shades around
me creep
As now I lay me down
to sleep.

I pray Thee, Lord,
my soul to keep
And while I wake or
while I sleep,
And while I work and while I play,
Give me Thy grace, that, day by day,
Thy love may in my heart
grow deep,
I pray Thee, Lord, my soul to keep.

If I should die before I wake;
If I this night the world forsake,
And leave the friends I hold most dear,
Leave all that I so value here;
And if Thy call my slumbers break—
If I should die before I wake,

I pray Thee, Lord, my soul to take;
I pray that Thou wouldst for me make
Close to Thy feet a lovely place,
Where I may e'er behold Thy face,
And this I ask for Thy dear sake—
I pray Thee, Lord, my soul to take.

While bending at my Mother's knee,
This little prayer she taught to me—
"Now I lay me down to sleep,
I pray Thee, Lord, my soul to keep;
If I should die before I wake
I pray Thee, Lord, my soul to take."

The Star

By Jane Taylor

Twinkle, twinkle, little star,
How I wonder what you are!
Up above the world so high,
Like a diamond in the sky.

When the blazing sun is set,
When the grass with dew is wet,
Then you show your little light,
Twinkle, twinkle, all the night.

Then the traveler in the dark
Thanks you for your tiny spark;
He could not see which way to go
If you did not twinkle so.

In the dark blue sky you keep,
And often through the curtains peep,

For you never shut your eye
Till the sun is in the sky.

As your bright and tiny spark
Lights the traveler in the dark,
Though I know not what you are,
Twinkle, twinkle, little star.

September

Author Unknown

From Book Three of the New Education Readers

The goldenrod is yellow;
The corn is turning brown;
The trees in apple orchards
With fruit are bending down.

The gentians' bluest fringes
Are curling in the sun;
The dusty pads of milkweed
Its hidden silk has spun.

The sedges flaunt their harvest
In every meadow nook;

The asters by the brookside
Make asters in the brook.

From dewy lanes at morning,
The grapes' sweet odors rise;
At noon the roads all flutter
With yellow butterflies.

By all these lovely tokens
September days are here,
With summer's best of weather,
And autumn's best of cheer.

Trees

By Joyce Kilmer

I think that I shall never see
A poem lovely as a tree.

A tree whose hungry mouth is pressed
Against the earth's sweet
flowing breast;

A tree that looks at God all day
And lifts her leafy arms to pray;

A tree that may in summer wear
A nest of robins in her hair;

Upon whose bosom snow has lain;
Who intimately lives with rain.

Poems are made by fools like me,
But only God can make a tree.

The Swing

By Robert Louis Stevenson

How do you like to go up in a swing,
Up in the air so blue?
Oh, I do think it the pleasantest thing
Ever a child can do!

Up in the air and over the wall,
Till I can see so wide,
Rivers and trees and cattle and all,
Over the countryside—

Till I look down on the garden green,
Down on the roof so brown—
Up in the air I go flying again,
Up in the air and down!

The Duel
By Eugene Field

The gingham dog and the calico cat
Side by side on the table sat;
'Twas half past twelve, and (What do you think!)
Nor one nor t'other had slept a wink!
The old Dutch clock and the Chinese plate
Appeared to know as sure as fate
There was going to be a terrible spat.
(I wasn't there; I simply state
What was told to me by the Chinese plate!)

The gingham dog went "bow-wow-wow!"
And the calico cat replied "me-ow!"
The air was littered, an hour or so,
With bits of gingham and calico,
While the old Dutch clock in the chimney place
Up with its hands before its face,
For it always dreaded a family row!
(Now mind: I'm only telling you
What the old Dutch clock declares is true!)

The Chinese plate looked very blue,
And wailed, "Oh dear! what shall we do?"
But the gingham dog and the calico cat
Wallowed this way and tumbled that,
Employing every tooth and claw
In the awfullest way you ever saw—
And, oh! how the gingham and calico flew!
(Don't fancy I exaggerate—
I got my news from the Chinese plate!)

Next morning where the two had sat,
They found no trace of dog or cat;
And some folks think unto this day
That burglars stole the pair away!
But the truth about the cat and pup
Is this: They ate each other up!
Now what do you really think of that!
(The old Dutch clock it told me so,
And that is how I came to know.)

Little Boy Blue

By Eugene Field

The little toy dog is covered with dust,
But sturdy and staunch he stands;
The little toy soldier is red with rust,
And his musket molds in his hands.
Time was when the little toy dog was new,
And the soldier was passing fair;
And that was the time when our Little Boy Blue
Kissed them and put them there.

"Now, don't you go till I come," he said,
"And don't you make any noise!"
So, toddling off to his trundle bed,
He dreamt of the pretty toys;
And, as he was dreaming, an angel song
Awakened our Little Boy Blue—
Oh! the years are many, the years are long,
But the little toy friends are true!

Aye, faithful to Little Boy Blue they stand,
Each in the same old place,
Awaiting the touch of a little hand,
The smile of a little face;

And they wonder, as waiting the long years through,
In the dust of that little chair,
What has become of our Little Boy Blue,
Since he kissed them and put them there.

Put My Little Shoes Away

Author Unknown

Mother dear, come bathe my forehead
For I'm growing very weak,
Mama, let one drop of water
Fall upon my burning cheek;
Tell my loving little playmates

That I never more shall play.
Give them all my toys, but Mother,
Put my little shoes away.

You will do this, Mother, won't you,
Put my little shoes away?
Give them all my toys, but Mother,
Put my little shoes away.

Santa Claus, he brought them to me
With a lot of other things
And I think he brought an angel
With a pair of golden wings.
Now soon I will be an angel
By perhaps another day
So please, my dearest Mother,
Put my little shoes away.

Little Orphant Annie

By James Whitcomb Riley

Little Orphant Annie's come to our house to stay,
An' wash the cups an' saucers up, an' brush the
   crumbs away,
An' shoo the chickens off the porch, an' dust the
   hearth, an' sweep,
An' make the fire, an' bake the bread, an' earn
   her board-an'-keep;
An' all us other children, when the supper things
   is done,
We set around the kitchen fire an' has the
   mostest fun
A-list'nin' to the witch-tales 'at Annie tells
   about,
An' the Gobble-uns 'at gits you

   Ef you
         Don't
               Watch
                     Out!

Onc't they was a little boy wouldn't say his
   prayers,—
So when he went to bed at night, away upstairs,
His Mammy heerd him holler, an' his Daddy
   heerd him bawl,
An' when they turn't the kivvers down, he
   wasn't there at all!
An' they seeked him in the rafter-room, an'
   cubby-hole, an' press,
An' seeked him up the chimbly-flue, an'
   ever'wheres, I guess;
But all they ever found was thist his pants an'
   roundabout—
An' the Gobble-uns'll git you

   Ef you
         Don't
               Watch
                     Out!

An' one time a little girl 'ud allus laugh an' grin,
An' make fun of ever'one, an' all her blood an' kin;
An onc't, when they was "company," an' ole
   folks was there,
She mocked 'em an' shocked 'em, an' said she
   didn't care!
An' thist as she kicked her heels, and turn't to
   run an' hide,
They wuz two great big Black Things a-standin'
   by her side,
An' they snatched her through the ceilin' 'fore
   she knowed what she's about!
An' the Gobble-uns'll git you

   Ef you
         Don't
               Watch
                     Out!

An' little Orphant Annie says when the blaze
   is blue,
An' the lamp-wick sputters, an' the wind goes
   woo-oo!
An' you hear the crickets quit, an' the moon is
   gray,
An' the lightnin'-bugs in dew is all squenched
   away,—
You better mind yer parents, an' yer teachers
   fond an' dear,
An' churish them 'at loves you, an dry the
   orphant's tear,
An' he'p the pore an' needy ones 'at clusters all
   about,
Er the Gobble-uns'll git you

   Ef you
         Don't
               Watch
                     Out!

When We Were Children

By Frederick E. Weatherly

Have you forgotten, little wife,
Our far-off childhood's golden life?
Our splendid castles on the sands,
The boat I made with my own hands,

The rain that caught us in the wood,
The cakes we had when we were good,
The doll I broke and made you cry,
When we were children you and I!

Have you forgotten, little wife,
The dawning of that other life?
The strange new light the whole world wore,
When life love's perfect blossom bore!

The dreams we had! the songs we made!
The sunshine! and the woven shade!
The tears of many a sad good-bye,
When we were parted, you and I!

Ah, nay! your loving heart, I know,
Remembers still the long-ago;
It is the light of childhood's days
That shines through all your winning ways.

God grant we ne'er forget our youth,
Its innocence, and faith, and truth,
The smiles, the tears, and hopes gone by,
When we were children, you and I.

The Land of Make-Believe

Author Unknown

In the happy land of make-believe,
All dreams come true they say;
So take me back to that land tonight
As a carefree child at play.
Show me in the land of make-believe
The old Pandora box,
Where troubles and cares are put away.
And happiness seals the locks.
Sing me, in the land of make-believe
While weary teardrops start,
The childish songs I love to hear
And soothe my aching heart.

School Days

Author Unknown

Nothing to do, Nellie darling? Nothing to do,
  you say?
Let's take a trip on memory ship, back to the
  bygone days.
Sail to the old village schoolhouse, anchor
  outside the school door,
Look in and see—there's you and there's me,
  a couple of kids once more.

Chorus:
School days, school days, dear old golden rule days,
Reading and writing and 'rithmetic, taught to the
  tune of a hickory stick!

You were my queen in calico, I was your bashful,
  barefoot beau.
You wrote on my slate, "I love you, Joe," when
  we were a couple of kids.

"'Member the hill, Nellie darling?
An the oak tree that grows on its brow?
They've built forty stories upon that old hill, and
  the oak tree's an old chestnut now—
'Member the meadow so green, dear? So
  fragrant with clover and maize?
Into new city lots and preferred business plots,
  they're cutting up since those days.

Just For Fun

Chapter Two

I guess what won me over to a love of poetry was the first time I heard a dramatic recitation of "Casey at the Bat." I loved baseball. Along with most other boys of my age, I played it with passion. My father and I listened to games on the old Philco radio from far-off St. Louis. I envisioned myself as the next Ruth or Gehrig.

"Casey at the Bat" (printed on page 30) taught me just how much fun there could be within the lines of a poem. I laughed at the arrogance he displayed while watching the first two strikes streak over the plate. And, having been the last out in a sandlot game more than my share of times, I agonized with the hometown hero as "mighty Casey" struck out.

Another poem that caught my fancy was "The Monkey's Disgrace." Penned by an unnamed author, it took to task the Darwinian theory of evolution that was already bringing controversy to schools, pulpits and homes back in the Good Old Days. Raised in the "Bible Belt," I laughed with derision as the monkeys examined the possibility that man descended from their kind. I think the philosophical side of me was born in the chimps' examination of the seamier side of humanity.

Within the pages of this chapter, you will find a lot to smile about. From the whimsical to the ridiculous, you will be reminded of the days when many of Mother's favorite verses were read just for fun.

—Ken Tate

The Monkey's Disgrace

Author Unknown

Three monkeys sat in a coconut tree
Discussing things as they are said to be.
Said one to the others, "Now listen you two,
There's a rumor around that can't be true—
That man descended from our noble race;
The very idea is a great disgrace.

"No monkey has ever deserted his wife,
Starved her babies and ruined her life.
And you've never known a mother monk
To leave her babies with others to bunk,
Or pass from one on to another
'Till they scarcely know who is their mother.

"And another thing you'll never see—
A monk build a fence around a coconut tree,
Forbidding all other monks a taste.
And let the coconuts go to waste.
Why, if I'd put a fence around the tree,
Starvation would force you to steal from me!

"Here's another thing a monkey won't do—
Go out at night and get on a stew
Or use a gun or club or knife
To take some other monkey's life.
Yes, man descended, the ornery cuss,
But brother, he didn't descend from us."

The Preacher and the Bear

Author Unknown

A preacher went out hunting,
Was on a Sunday morn;
Of course it was against his religion,
But he took a gun along.

He shot himself some quail
And one little measly hare,
But on his way returning home
He met a great big bear.

Well, the bear got down in the middle of the road,
On all fours like a great big toad;
He looked that preacher right square in the eye;
The preacher looked at him and said, "Bye, bye."

He started down the road, took out to run,
The bear right after that preacher did come;
They run, and then run for about a mile,
They both sat down and rested for awhile.

The preacher got up and stirred again,
The bear he started out with more vim,
They run and they run 'till he spotted a tree,
Said, "Up on the limb, there's a place for me."

The bear reached out, made a grab for him;
The preacher leaped up and made the limb,
Pulled himself up and turned about,
Cast his eyes to the skies and he did
    shout:

Chorus
O Lord, you delivered Daniel from the
    lion's den,
Also delivered Jonah from the whale,
    and then
The Hebrew children in the fiery
    furnace,
So the Good Book do declare,
Lord, if you can't help me,
For goodness sake don't help that bear!

Just about then the limb came loose
And the preacher came tumbling down.
He reached in his pocket and pulled his razor out
Just before he hit the ground.

He hit the ground with an awful bang;
It was a terrible sight,
The preacher and the bear, with the razor in his hair,
Just a-cutting left and right.

He thought, if I'd get out of here alive,
That Good Book I will abide;
I'll never sin on Sabbath day,
And Sunday come I'll pray and pray.

To the Heavens he did glance,
Said, "Lord, just give me one more chance."
Then his suspenders gave away
And he knocked that bear ten feet away.

Got up and turned around
To a tree where he'd be safe and sound
Pulled himself up and turned about,
Cast his eyes to the skies and he did shout:

Chorus

The Old Maid's Burglar

Author Unknown

A story I'll tell of a
  burglar bold
 Who started to rob a
house.
 He opened the window,
And then crept in as quiet
as a mouse.

He looked around for a
  place to hide
    Till the folks were
  all asleep,
      And then, said
  he, "With their
  money
        I'll take a
        quiet
         sneak."

So under the bed the burglar crept,
He crept up close to the wall;
He didn't know it was an old maid's room
Or he wouldn't have had the gall.

He thought of the money that he would steal
As under the bed he lay,
But at nine o'clock he saw a sight
That made his hair turn gray.

At nine o'clock the old maid came in;
"I am so tired," she said.
She thought that all was well that night,
So she didn't look under the bed.

She took out her teeth and her big glass eye
And the hair all off her head;
The burglar, he had forty fits
As he watched from under the bed.

From under the bed the burglar crept
He was a total wreck;
The old maid wasn't asleep at all
And she grabbed him by the neck.

She didn't holler, or shout, or call,
She was as cool as a clam;
She only said, "The Saints be praised!
At last I've got a man."

From under the pillow a gun she drew
And to the burglar she said,
"Young man, if you don't marry me,
I'll blow off the top of your head."

She held him firmly by the neck,
He hadn't a chance to scoot;
He looked at the teeth and the big glass eye
And said, "Madam, for Pete's sake, shoot!"

I Wish I Were Single Again

Author Unknown

When I was single, oh then, oh then,
When I was single, oh then—
When I was single
My pockets did jingle,
And I wish I were single again.

I got me a wife, oh then, oh then,
I got me a wife, oh then,
I got me a wife,
She was plague of my life,
And I wish I were single again.

My wife she died, oh then, oh then,
My wife she died, oh then;
My wife she died
And I laughed till I cried
To think I was single again.

I married another, oh then, oh then,
I married another, oh then;
I married another
She's the devil's stepmother,
And I wish I were single again.

She beat me, she banged me, oh
  then, oh then,
She beat me, she banged me, oh then;
She beat me, she banged me,
She swore she would hang me,
And I wish I were single again.

She got the rope, oh then, oh then,
She got the rope, oh then;
She got the rope,
My neck it did choke,
And I wish I were single again.

The limb did break, oh then, oh then,
The limb did break, oh then,
The limb did break,
My neck did escape,
And I wish I were single again.

Young men take warning from this,
  oh this;
Young men taking warning from this—
Be good to the first,
For the last is much worse.
And you'll wish you were single again.

I Had But Fifty Cents

By Jimmy Long

I took my girl to a fancy ball,
It was a social hop,
We stayed until the folks went home,
And till the music stopped.
Then to a restaurant we went,
The best one on the street,
She said she wasn't hungry,
But this is what she ate.

One dozen raw, a plate of slaw,
A chicken and a roast,
Some asparagus and applesauce,
And soft-shell crabs and toast.
An Irish stew and crackers too,
Her appetite was immense,
When she called for pie,
I tho't I'd die,
For I had but fifty cents.

She said she wasn't hungry,
She didn't come to eat,
I'll bet my only trousers,
That she cannot be beat.
She said everything was rosy,
She had an awful tank,
She said she wasn't thirsty,
But this is what she drank.

A whiskey skin, a glass of gin,
It made me shake with fear,
Some ginger pop with rum on top,
And then a glass of beer.
A glass of ale, a gin cocktail,
She should have had more sense,
When she called for more, I fell on the floor,
For I had but fifty cents.

You bet I wasn't hungry,
I didn't care to eat,
Expecting every moment to be
Kicked out in the street.
She said she'd bring her family in,
And we would have some fun.
I gave the man the fifty cents,
And this is what he done.

He tore my clothes, he smashed
     my nose,
He hit me more and more.
He gave me two black eyes
And with me swept the floor.
He took me by my trousers
And threw me o'er fence.
Take my advice, don't try it twice,
When you've got but fifty cents.

Flour-Sack Underwear

By Ruth Gettle

When I was a maiden, fair
Mama made our underwear.
With five tots and Pa's poor pay,
How could she buy lingerie?
Monograms and fancy stitches
Were not on our flour-sack britches.
Panty waists that stood the test,
With "Gold Medal" on the chest.

Little pants the best of all,
With a scene I still recall:
Harvesters were gleaning wheat,
Right across the little seat.

Tougher than a grizzly bear
Was our flour-sack underwear;
Plain or fancy, three feet wide,
Stronger than a hippo's hide.

Through the years each Jill and Jack,
Wore this sturdy garb of sack
Waste not, want not, we soon learned,
Penny saved, a penny earned.
Bedspreads, curtains, tea towels too,
Tablecloths to name a few.
But the best beyond compare,
Was our flour-sack underwear.

Me and Betsy

By Will Carleton

In a pioneer's cabin, out West, so they say,
A great big black grizzly trotted one day.
And, seating himself on the hearth, he began
To lap up the contents of a two-gallon pan
Of milk and potatoes. An excellent meal.
He then looked about to see what else he
    could steal.

The lord of the mansion awoke from his sleep,
And hearing a racket, he ventured to peep,
Just out in the kitchen, to see what was there,
And was scared to behold a great grizzly bear.
He screamed in alarm to his slumbering frau,
"There's a bar in the kitchen, as big as a cow!"
"A what?" "Why a bar!" "Well, slaughter him then."
"I will my brave Betsy, if you'll first venture in."

So Betsy leaped up, and the poker she seized,
While her man shut the door, and against it, he
    squeezed.
While Betsy laid hard on the grizzly her blows,

"Now on the forehead! Now on the nose!"
Her man through the keyhole kept shouting
    with vim.
"Well done, my brave Betsy! Now hit 'im agin!
A rap on the ribs and a knock on the snout.
Now poke with the poker and poke his eyes out!"
So with rapping and poking, poor Betsy alone,
At last had Sir Bruin as dead as a stone.
And when the old man saw that the bear was
    no more,
He ventured to poke his nose, just out of the door,
And there lay the grizzly, stretched out on the floor.

Then off to the neighbors he hastened to tell
All the wonderful things that morning'd befell.
He published the marvelous story afar,
How "Me and my Betsy just slaughtered a bar!
Oh, yes! Come and see! All the neighbors have
    seen it.
Come and see what we did! Me and Betsy, we
    did it!"

The Barefoot Boy With Boots On

Author Unknown

'Twas midnight on the ocean,
Not a streetcar was in sight,
The sun was shining brightly,
It rained all day that night.

It was evening and the rising sun
Was setting in the west,
Little fishes in the trees
Were budding in their nests.

The organ peeled potatoes,
Lard was rendered by the choir,
The sexton rang the dishrag,
Someone set the house on fire.

"Holy Smoke!" the preacher shouted,
As in the rain he lost his hair,
And now his head resembles heaven,
As there is no parting there.

The lightning struck the cowshed,
The cows all chewing their cud,
The moonlight set the prairie on fire,
Out in the middle of the woods.

The barefoot boy with boots on,
Came crawling down the street,
His pants were full of pockets,
His shoes were full of feet.

He was born when he was a baby,
His grandmother's pride and joy,
His only sister was a girl,
His brother was a boy.

He never was a triplet,
Came one of being twins;
His legs were fastened to his knees,
Just above his shins.

His hands were fastened to his arms,
Seven inches from his shoulders,
When he was grown he was a man,
Every day he got older.

One day he married a woman,
Who quickly became his wife,
He couldn't stay single,
So he lived a married life.

His wife was full of notion,
Her mouth was full of tongue;
They raised a dozen children,
All born when they were young.

They had six girls and five boys
And then, another child.
They didn't try to tame them,
Just let them grow up wild.

The young one was the baby,
The old one was born first,
The good one was the best one,
And the mean one was the worst.

They never knew their ages,
They didn't seem to care,
They knew they had a birthday,
Coming every year.

They didn't know their father's age,
But always had a hunch,
That he was born before the rest,
And the oldest of the bunch.

When they died, they could not speak,
Their names they could not tell,
The girls all went to heaven
And the boys all went—oh well!

The Barefoot Boy With Boots On

Version Two
Author Unknown

Editor's Note: *As with so many of the folks songs of our past, there were several versions of "The Barefoot Boy With Boots On." At first we thought of consolidating the different verses into one version that would be representative, but after coming across this very different rendition, thought we would share both with you.—K.T.*

The night was dark and dreary,
The sun was shining bright.
The stars were casting brilliant rays
On the storm that raged that night.

The lightning hit the cowshed,
The cows all chewed their cud.
The moonlight set the prairie on fire
In the middle of a flood.

The barefoot boy with boots on
Lay standing in the street.
His pants were full of pockets,
His boots were full of feet.

He was born when just a baby,
His grandma's pride and joy.
His only sister was a girl;
His brother was a boy.

He never knew his father's age,
But always had a hunch
That he was born before the one
That was oldest of the bunch.

He never was a triplet,
But always was a twin.
His legs were fastened to his knees
Just above the shin.

His teeth were fastened in his head
Several inches from his shoulder.
When he grew up he was a man
And every day got older.

One day he married a woman
Who soon became his wife.
Her weight was just 600;
She weighed that all her life.

Her head was full of blond hair,
Her mouth was full of tongue.
They raised a dozen children,
All born when they were young.

The youngest was the baby,
The oldest was born first,
The good one was the best one,
And the bad one was the worst.

They never knew their ages
But never had to fear;
They knew they had a birthday
A-coming every year.

And when they died they could not speak,
Their names they could not tell.
The girls all went to heaven;
Where the boys went, I won't tell.

Four Thousand Years Ago

Author Unknown

I was born about four thousand years ago,
And there's nothing in this world that I don't know,
I saw Jonah swallow the whale,
And I pulled the lion's tail
And I'll whip the man who says it isn't so.

So you see I am an educated man.
To keep my brain within my head I plan,
I've been on this earth so long,
That I used to sing a song,
While Abraham and Isaac rushed the can.

I have sat with Kings and Queens on every hand,
Jacks and Aces can't you understand,
And I saw the flags a-flying
When George Washington stopped lying,
And I swear I was the man who led the band.

I saw Eve when she searched the garden o'er,
I saw Satan when they drove him from the door,
While the apple they were eating
From the bushes I was peeping,
And I'll swear I was the man who ate the core.

I saw Sampson when he laid the village cold,
I saw Daniel tame the lions in the hold,
I helped build the Tower of Babel,
Just as high as we were able,
And there's lots of other things I haven't told.

I taught Solomon his little ABCs,
I helped Brigham Young to make Limburger cheese,
And while sailing down the bay,
With Methuselah one day,
I saved his flowing whiskers from the breeze.

Queen Elizabeth she fell in love with me,
We were married in Milwaukee secretly,
But I fooled around and shook 'er,
And went with General Hooker,
To shoot mosquitoes down in Tennessee.

I remember when this country had a king,
I saw Cleopatra pawn her wedding ring,
I saw Peter, Paul, and Moses,
Playing ring-a-round-the-roses,
On the night when Patti first began to sing.

I saw Noah when he built his famous Ark,
And I crept into it one night in the dark,
I saw Old King Pharaoh's daughter
Rescue Moses from the water,
And I crossed the River Canaan on a lark.

I saw Cain when he slew Abel in the glade,
And I knew the game was poker that they played,
And so right there was a rub,
Did he kill him with a club?
No, I'm sure it was a diamond or a spade.

I'm My Own Grandpa

By Dwight Latham and Moe Jaffe

Many years ago
When I was twenty-three
I was married to a widow,
Who was as pretty as could be.
The widow had a grown-up daughter
Who had hair of red,
And my father fell in love with her
And soon they were wed.
This made my father my son-in-law
And changed my very life,
For my daughter was my mother
Since she was my father's wife.

To complicate the matter
Even though it brought me joy,
I soon became the father
Of a bouncing baby boy.
My little baby then became
A brother-in-law to Dad,
And so became my uncle
Though that made me sad,
For if he was my uncle
That also made him a brother,
Of the widow's grown-up daughter,
Who was, of course,
My stepmother.

Now my father's wife then had a son
Who kept them on the run,
And he became my grandchild
For he was my daughter's son.
My wife is now my mother's mother
And that makes me blue,
Because although she is my wife
She is my grandmother, too.
Oh! If my wife is my grandmother,
Then I am her grandchild,
And every time I think of it,
It nearly drives me wild.

For now I have become
The strangest case I ever saw,
As husband of my grandmother,
I am my own grandpa!

Casey at the Bat

By Ernest L. Thayer

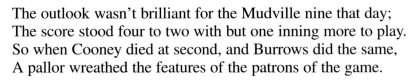

The outlook wasn't brilliant for the Mudville nine that day;
The score stood four to two with but one inning more to play.
So when Cooney died at second, and Burrows did the same,
A pallor wreathed the features of the patrons of the game.

A straggling few got up to go in deep despair. The rest
Clung to the hope which springs eternal in the human breast;
They thought, "If only Casey could but get a whack at that—
We'd put up even money now, with Casey at the bat."

But Flynn preceded Casey, as did also Jimmy Blake,
And the former was a lulu and the latter was a fake;
So upon that stricken multitude a deathlike silence sat,
For there seemed but little chance of Casey's getting to the bat.

But Flynn let drive a single, to the wonderment of all,
And Blake, the much despised, tore the cover off the ball;
And when the dust had lifted, and they saw what had occurred,
There was Jimmy safe at second, and Flynn a-hugging third.

Then from five thousand throats and more there rose a lusty yell;
It rumbled in the mountaintops, it rattled in the dell;
It knocked upon the hillside and recoiled upon the flat;
For Casey, mighty Casey, was advancing to the bat.

There was ease in Casey's manner as he stepped into his place;
There was pride in Casey's bearing and a smile on Casey's face.
And when, responding to the cheers, he lightly doffed his hat,
No stranger in the crowd could doubt 'twas Casey at the bat.

Ten thousand eyes were on him as he rubbed his hands with dirt;
Five thousand tongues applauded when he wiped them on his shirt.
Then while the writhing pitcher ground the ball into his hip,
Defiance gleamed in Casey's eye, a sneer curled Casey's lip.

And now the leather-covered sphere came hurtling through the air,
And Casey stood a-watching it in haughty grandeur there.
Close by the sturdy batsman the ball unheeded sped—
"That ain't my style," said Casey—"Strike one," the Umpire said.

From the benches black with people, there went up a muffled roar,
Like the beating of the storm-waves on a stern and distant shore.
"Kill him! Kill the umpire!" shouted someone on the stand;
And it's likely they'd have killed him had not Casey raised his hand.

With a smile of Christian charity great Casey's visage shone;
He stilled the rising tumult; he bade the game go on;
He signaled to the pitcher, and once more the spheroid flew;
But Casey still ignored it, and the Umpire said, "Strike two."

"Fraud!" cried the maddened thousands, and the echo answered, "Fraud!"
But one scornful look from Casey, and the multitude was awed.
They saw his face grow stern and cold, they saw his muscles strain,
And they knew that Casey wouldn't let that ball go by again.

The sneer is gone from Casey's lip, his teeth are clenched in hate;
He pounds with cruel violence his bat upon plate.
And now the pitcher holds the ball, and now he lets it go,
And now the air is shattered by the force of Casey's blow.

Oh, somewhere in this favored land the sun is shining bright;
The band is playing somewhere, and somewhere hearts are light,
And somewhere men are laughing, and somewhere children shout;
But there is no joy in Mudville—mighty Casey has struck out.

Wynken, Blynken and Nod

By Eugene Field

Wynken, Blynken, and Nod one night
Sailed off in a wooden shoe—
Sailed on a river of crystal light,
Into a sea of dew.
"Where are you going, and what do you
    wish?"
The old moon asked the three.
"We have come to fish for the herring fish
That live in this beautiful sea;
Nets of silver and gold have we!"
   Said Wynken,
      Blynken,
         And Nod.

The old moon laughed and sang a song,
As they rocked in the wooden shoe,
And the wind that sped them all night long
Ruffled the waves of dew.
The little stars were the herring fish
That lived in that beautiful sea—
"Now cast your nets wherever you wish—
Never afeared are we!"
So cried the stars to the fisherman three:
   Wynken,
      Blynken,
         And Nod.

All night long their nets they threw
To the stars in the twinkling foam—
Then down from the skies came the wooden shoe,
Bringing the fishermen home;
'T was all so pretty a sail it seemed
As if it could not be,
And some folks thought 't was a dream
    they'd dreamed
Of sailing that beautiful sea—
But I shall name you the fishermen three:
   Wynken,
      Blynken,
         And Nod.

Wynken and Blynken are two little eyes,
And Nod is a little head,
And the wooden shoe that sailed the skies
Is a wee one's trundle-bed.
So shut your eyes while mother sings
Of wonderful sights that be,
And you shall see the beautiful things
As you rock in the misty sea,
Where the old shoe rocked the fisherman three:
   Wynken,
      Blynken,
         And Nod.

My Get-Up-And-Go

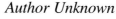

Author Unknown

How do I know my youth is all spent?
Well, my get-up-and-go just got up and went,
But in spite of it all, I'm able to grin
When I think of where my get-up has been.

Old age is golden, so I've heard it said,
But sometimes I wonder as I get into bed,
With my ears in a drawer, my teeth in a cup,
My eyes on the table until I wake up.

Ere sleep dims my eyes—I say to myself,
"Is there anything else should have laid on
   the shelf?"
But I am happy to say as I close my door,
My friends are the same, perhaps even more.

When I was young, my slippers were red,
And I could kick my heels right over my head;
When I grew older, my slippers were blue,
And I could dance the whole night through.

Now, I am old, my slippers are black;
I walk to the corner and then I walk back.
The reason I know my youth is all spent
Is my get-up-and-go just got up and went.

But I really don't mind when I think with a grin
Of all the places my get-up has been.
Since I've retired from life's competition,
I busy myself with complete repetition.

I get up each morning, dust off my wits,
Pick up the paper and read the obits,
If my name is missing, I know I'm not dead,
So I eat a good breakfast and go back to bed.

When Father Carves the Duck

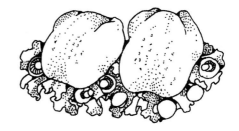

By E.V. Wright

We all look on with anxious eyes
When Father carves the duck,
And Mother almost always sighs
When Father carves the duck.
Then all of us prepare to rise,
And hold our bibs before our eyes,
And be prepared for some surprise,
When Father carves the duck.

He braces up and grabs a fork,
Whene'er he carves a duck,
And won't allow a soul to talk,
Until he's carved the duck.
The fork is jabbed into the sides,
Across the breast the knife he slides,
While every careful person hides
From flying chips of duck.

The platter's always sure to slip,
When Father carves a duck.
And how it makes the dishes skip!
Potatoes fly amuck!
The squash and cabbage leap in space,
We get some gravy in our face,
And Father mutters Hindoo grace,
Whene'er he carves a duck.

We all have learned to walk around
The dining room and pluck
From off the window sills and walls
Our share of Father's duck.
While Father growls and blows and jaws,
And swears the knife was full of flaws,
And Mother jeers at him because
He cannot carve a duck.

Old Favorites

My wife Janice and I have worked with *Good Old Days* magazine for well over a decade. One of the great pleasures we have had in all those years is helping hundreds of folks find the words to poems and songs they remember from their youth.

We have always been amazed at how folks from all over North America remember lines from dozens and dozens of poems I would call "Old Favorites." We knew we would have to have a chapter devoted to at least a sampling of verse that so many of our readers remember and request over and over again.

One such old favorite for me was one I didn't understand when I was a child. Both my grandmothers had lost children in infancy, and one—I don't remember which—would recite "Little Half-Worn Shoes." I thought the verse was talking about the shoes of one of my uncles or aunts that were set back as keepsakes.

I never understood the melancholy the poem brought to them as they recited it. Years later I found that the poem reminded them of the hole left in their heart with the loss of such a precious little life.

That is the wonderful side to poetry. It has the ability to awaken emotions long asleep in our souls. I know your emotions will run the gamut of joy and pain, mirth and melancholy as they are awakened by these Old Favorites.

—Ken Tate

Little Half-Worn Shoes *Author Unknown*

God bless the little feet that never go astray,
For the little shoes are empty, in my closet laid away.
Sometimes I take one in my hand forgetting till I see
It is a half-worn shoe, not large enough for me;
And at once I feel a sense of bitter loss and pain
As sharp as when two years ago it cut my heart in twain.

Oh, little feet that wearied not, I wait for them no more,
For I am drifting on the tide, but they have reached the shore.
And while the blinding teardrops wet these little shoes so old,
I try to think my darling's feet are treading streets of gold;
And I lay them down again, but always turn to say,
"God bless the little feet that now so surely cannot stray."

The House by the Side of the Road

By Sam Walter Foss

There are hermit souls that live withdrawn
In the place of their self-content;
There are souls like stars, that dwell apart,
In a fellowless firmament;
There are pioneer souls that blaze their paths
Where highways never ran—
But let me live by the side of the road
And be a friend to man.

Let me live in a house by the side of the road,
Where the race of men go by—
The men who are good and the men who are bad,
As good and as bad as I.
I would not sit in the scorner's seat,
Nor hurl the cynic's ban—
Let me live in a house by the side of the road
And be a friend to man.

I see from my house by the side of the road,
By the side of the highway of life,
The men who press with the ardor of hope,
The men who are faint with the strife.
But I turn not away from their smiles nor their tears,
Both parts of an infinite plan—
Let me live in a house by the side of the road
And be a friend to man.

I know there are brook-gladdened meadows ahead,
And mountains of wearisome height;
That the road passes on through the long afternoon
And stretches away to the night.
But still I rejoice when the travelers rejoice,
And weep with the strangers that moan,
Nor live in my house by the side of the road
Like a man who dwells alone.

Let me live in my house by the side of the road,
It's here the race of men go by—
They are good, they are bad, they are weak, they are strong,
Wise, foolish—so am I;
Then why should I sit in the scorner's seat,
Or hurl the cynic's ban?
Let me live in my house by the side of the road
And be a friend to man.

When the Frost Is on the Punkin

By James Whitcomb Riley

When the frost is on the punkin and the fodder's in the shock,
And you hear the kyouck and gobble of the struttin' turkey-cock,
And the clackin' of the guineas and the cluckin' of the hens,
And the rooster's hallylooyer as he tiptoes on the fence,
O, it's then's the times a feller is a-feelin' at his best,
With the risin' sun to greet him from a night of peaceful rest,
As he leaves the house, bareheaded, and goes out to feed the stock,
When the frost is on the punkin and the fodder's in the shock.

They's something kindo' harty-like about the atmusfere
When the heat of summer' over and the coolin' fall is here—
Of course we miss the flowers, and the blossoms on the trees,
And the mumble of the hummin'-birds and buzzin' of the bees;
But the air's so appetizin'; and the landscape through the haze
Of a crisp and sunny morning of the airly autumn days
Is a pictur' that no painter has the colorin' to mock—
When the frost is on the punkin and the fodder's in the shock.

The husky, rusty russel of the tossels of the corn,
And the raspin' of the tangled leaves, as golden as the morn;
The stubble in the furries—kindo' lonesome-like, but still
A-preachin' sermons to us of the barns they growed to fill;
The strawstack in the medder, and the reaper in the shed;
The hosses in theyr stalls below—the clover overhead!—
O, it sets my hart a-clickin' like the tickin' of a clock,
When the frost is on the punkin and the fodder's in the shock!

Then your apples all is gethered, and the ones a feller keeps
Is poured around the cellar-floor in red and yeller heaps;
And your cider-makin's over and
your wimmern-folks is through
With their mince and apple-butter,
and theyr souse and saussage, too!
I don't know how to tell it—
but ef sich a thing could be
As the Angels wantin' boardin',
and they call around on me—
I'd want to 'commodate' em
all the whole-indurin' flock—
When the frost is on the punkin
and the fodder's in the shock.

The Little Match Girl *Author Unknown*

Little Gretchen, little Gretchen wanders up and down the street;
The snow is on her yellow hair, the frost is at her feet,
The rows of long, dark houses, without, look cold and damp,
By the struggling of the moonbeam, by the flicker of the lamp,
The clouds ride fast as horses, the wind is from the north,
But no one cares for Gretchen and no one looketh forth.
Within those dark, damp houses are merry faces bright,
An happy hearts are watching out the old year's latest night.

With the little box of matches she could not sell all day,
And the thin, thin tattered mantle
the wind blows every way,
She clingeth to the railing, she shivers in the gloom—
There are parents sitting snugly
by the firelight in the room;
And children with grave faces
are whispering one another
Of present for the New Year, for father or for mother,
But no one talks to Gretchen,
and no one hears her speak,
No breath of little whispers
comes warmly to her cheek.

No little arms are round her.
Ah, me! that there should be,
With so much happiness on earth, so much of misery!
Sure they of many blessings
should scatter blessings round,
As fruit-trees in autumn fling
their ripe fruits to the ground,
And the best love man can offer to the God of love,
be sure,
Is kindness to His little ones, and bounty to the poor,
Little Gretchen, little Gretchen, goes coldly on her way;
There's no one looketh out at her,
there's no one bids her stay.

Her home is cold and desolate; no smile, no food, no fire,
But children clamorous for bread, and an impatient sire,
So she sits down in an angle where two great houses meet,
And she curleth up beneath her, for warmth, her little feet;
And she looketh on the cold wall, and on the colder sky,
And wonders if the little stars are bright fires up on high.
She hears a clock strike slowly, up in a far church-tower,
With such a sad and solemn tone, telling the midnight hour.

And she remembers of tales her mother used to tell,
And of the cradle songs she sang, when summer's twilight fell;
Of good men and angels, and of the Holy Child,
Who was cradled in a manger, when winter was most wild,
Who was poor, and cold, and hungry, and desolate and lone,
And she thought the song had told He was ever with His own;
And all the poor and hungry and forsaken ones are His.
"How good of Him to look on me in such a place as this."

Colder it grows, and colder, but she does not feel it now,
For the pressure at her heart, and the weight upon her brow;
But she struck one little match on the wall so cold and bare,
That she might look around her, and see if He were there.
The single match had kindled, and by the light it threw
It seemed to little Gretchen the wall was rent in two;
And she could see folks seated at a table richly spread,
With heaps of goodly viands, red wine and pleasant bread.

She could smell the fragrant savor, she could hear what they did say,
Then all was darkness once again, the match had burned away,
She struck another hastily, and now she seemed to see
Within the same warm chamber, a glorious Christmas-tree.
The branches were all laden with things that children prize,
Bright gifts for boys and maiden, she saw them with her eyes,
And she almost seemed to touch them, and to join the welcome shout,
When darkness fell around her, for the little match was out.

Another, yet another, she had tried—they will not light;
Till all her little store she took, and struck with all her might;
And the whole miserable place was lighted with the glare,
And she dreamed there stood a little child before her in the air,
There were blood-drops on His forehead, a spear-wound in His side,
And cruel nail-prints in His feet, and in His hands spread wide,
And He looked upon her gently, and she felt that He had known
Pain, hunger, cold and sorrow—ay, equal to her own.

And he pointed to the laden board and to the Christmas-tree,
Then up to the cold sky, and said: "Will Gretchen come with me?"
The poor child felt her pulses fall, she felt her eyeballs swim,
And a ringing sound was in her ears, like her dead mother's hymn;
Then folded both her thin, white hands, and turned from that bright board,
And from the golden gifts, and said:"With Thee, with Thee, O Lord!"
The chilly winter morning breaks up in the dull skies,
On the city wrapped in vapor, on the spot where Gretchen lies.

In her scant and tattered garment, with her back against the wall,
She sitteth cold and rigid, she answers no call.
They have lifted her up fearfully, they shuddered as they said:
"It was a bitter, bitter night; the child is frozen dead."
The angels sang their greeting for one more redeemed from sin;
Men said: "It was a bitter night; would no one let her in?"
And they shivered as they spoke of her, and sighed. They could not see
How much of happiness there was, after that misery.

Whistling in Heaven *Author Unknown*

You're surprised that I ever should say so?
Just wait till the reason I've given
Why I say I shan't care for the music,
Unless there is whistling in Heaven.
Then you'll think it no very great wonder
Not so strange, not so bold a conceit,
That unless there's a boy there a-whistling,
Its music will not be complete.

It was late in the autumn of '40
We had come from our far eastern home
Just in season to build us a cabin,
'Ere the cold of the winter should come;
And we lived all the while in our wagon
That husband was clearing the place
Where the house was to stand: and the clearing
And building it took many days.

So that our heads were scarce sheltered
In under its roof, when our store
Of provisions was almost exhausted
And husband must journey for more.
And the nearest place where he could get them
Was yet such a distance away,
That it forced him from home to be absent
At least a whole night and a day.

You see we'd but two or three neighbors,
And the nearest was more than a mile;
And we hadn't found time yet to know them,
For we had been busy the while.
And the man who'd helped at the raising,
Just stayed till the job was well done,
And as soon as his money was paid him,
Had shouldered his ax and had gone.

Well, husband just kissed me and started—
I could scarcely suppress a deep groan,
At the thought of remaining with baby,
So long in the house all alone,
For, my dear, I was childish and timid
And braver ones might well have feared,
For the wild wolf was often heard howling,
And savages sometimes appeared.

But I smothered my grief and my terror,
Till husband was off on his ride,
And then in my arms I took Josie,
And all the day long sat and cried,
As I thought of the long dreary hours
When the darkness of night should fall
And I was so utterly helpless
With no one in reach of my call.

And when the night came with its terror
To hide every ray of light,
I hung up a quilt by the window,
And almost dead with affright,
I kneeled by the side of the cradle
Scarce daring to draw a full breath,
Lest the baby should wake and its crying
Should bring us a horrible death.

There I knelt until late in the evening,
And scarcely an inch had I stirred,
When suddenly, far in the distance
A sound of whistling, I heard.
I started up dreadfully frightened
For fear 'twas an Indian's call,
And then very soon I remembered
The red man never whistles at all.

And when I was sure 'twas a white man
I thought, were he coming for ill,
He'd surely approach with more caution,
Would come without warning, and still.
Then the sounds, coming nearer and nearer,
Took the form of a tune light and gay
And I knew I needn't fear evil
From one who could whistle that way.

Very soon I heard footsteps approaching,
Then came a peculiar dull thump;
As if someone was heavily striking
An ax in the top of a stump
And then in another brief moment,
There come a light tap on the door
When quickly I undid the fastening
And in stepped a boy, and before

There was neither a question or answer
Or neither had time to speak,
I just threw my glad arms around him
And gave him a kiss on the cheek.
Then I started back, scared at my boldness
But he only smiled at my fright,
As he said, "I'm your neighbor's boy, Elick,
Come to tarry with you through the night.

"We saw your husband go eastward
And made up our minds where he'd gone,
And I said to the rest of our people,
'That woman is there all alone,
And I venture she's awfully lonesome,
And though she may have no great fear,
I think she would feel a bit safer
If only a boy were but near.'

"So, taking my ax on my shoulder,
For fear that a savage might stray
Across my path and need scalping,
I started right down this way,
And, coming in sight of the cabin,
And thinking to save you alarm,
I whistled a tune just to show you
I didn't intend any harm.

"And so here I am at your service:
But if you don't want me to stay,
Why all you need do is say so,
And should'ring my ax I'll away."
I dropped in a chair and near fainted
Just at thought of leaving me then,
And his eyes gave a knowing bright twinkle
And he said, "I guess I'll remain."

And then I just sat there and told him
How terribly frightened I'd been,
How his face was to me the most welcome
Of any I ever had seen.
And then I lay down with the baby,
And slept all the blessed night through,
For I felt I was safe from all danger
Near so brave a young fellow and true.

So now, my dear friend, do you wonder,
Since such a good reason I've given,
Why I say I shan't care for the music
Unless there is whistling in heaven?
Yes, often I've said so in earnest,
And now what I've said I'll repeat:
That unless there's a boy there whistling
Its music will not be complete.

May I Sleep in Your Barn Tonight?

Author Unknown

One night it was dark and was storming
When along came a tramp in the lane;
He was making his way to the station
To catch on to a long-distance train.

May I sleep in your barn tonight, mister?
It is cold lying out on the ground,
And the cold north wind it is whistling
And I have no place to lie down.

Oh, I have no tobacco or matches,
I assure you I'll do you no harm;
I will tell you my story, mister;
For it runs through my heart like a storm.

It was three years ago last summer—
I shall never forget that sad day—
When a stranger came out from the city
And said that he wanted to stay.

One night as I came from my workshop
I was whistling and singing with joy;
I expected a kind, hearty welcome
From my sweet, loving wife and my boy.

But what should I find but a letter,
It was placed in a room on a stand;
In a moment my eyes fell upon it
And I picked it right up in my hand.

Now this note said my wife and the stranger,
They had left and had taken my son;
Oh, I wonder if God up in Heaven
Only knows what this stranger has done.

Are All My Children In?

Author Unknown

I think of times as the night draws nigh—
Of an old house on the hill,
Of a yard all wide and blossomed, and starred;
Where the children played at will,
And when at last the night came down,
Hushing the merry din,
Mother would look around and ask,
"Are all my children in?"

'Tis many and many of years since then,
And the old house on the hill
No longer echoes to childish feet,
And the yard is still, so still,
And we see it all as the shadows creep,
And though many years have been
Since then, we can hear our mother ask,
"Are all my children in?"

I wonder if, when the shadows fall—
On the short earthly day,
When we say good-bye to the world outside,
All tired with our earthly play,
When we step into that other land—
Where our mother has gone,
Will we hear her ask just as of old,
"Are all my
   children in?"

The Lips That Touch Liquor Must Never Touch Mine

By Harriet A. Glazebrook

You are coming to woo me, but not as of yore,
When I hastened to welcome your ring at the door;
For I trusted that he who stood waiting me then,
Was the brightest, the truest, the noblest of men.
Your lips on my own when they printed "Farewell,"
Had never been soiled by the "beverage of Hell,"
But they come to me now with the bacchanal sign,
And the lips that touch liquor
    must never touch mine.

I think of that night
    in the garden alone,
When in whispers you told me
    your heart was my own,
That your love in the future
    should faithfully be
Unshared by another,
    kept only for me.
Oh, sweet to my soul
    is the memory still
Of the lips which met mine,
    when they whispered "I will";
But now to their pressure
    they no more incline,
For the lips that touch liquor must never
    touch mine.

Oh John! How it crushed me, when first in
    your face
The pen of the "Rum Fiend" had written "disgrace";
And turned me in silence
    and tears from that breath
All poisoned and foul from the chalice of death.
It scattered the hopes I had treasured to last;
It darkened the future and clouded the past;
It shattered my idol, and ruined the shrine,
For the lips that touch liquor must never touch mine.

I loved you—Oh, dearer than language can tell,
And you saw it, you proved it, you knew it too well!
But the man of my love was far other than he
Who now from the "Tap-room"
    comes reeling to me;
In manhood and honor so noble and right—
His heart was so true, and his genius so bright—
And his soul was unstained, unpolluted by wine;
        But the lips that touch liquor
            must never touch mine.

You promised reform,
    but I trusted in vain;
        Your pledge was but made
        to be broken again;
        And the lover so false
        to his promises now
        Will not as a husband
        be true to his vow.
        The word must be spoken that
        bids you depart—
        Though the effort to speak it
        should shatter my heart—
        Though in silence, with blighted
        affection, I pine,
Yet the lips that touch liquor
    must never touch mine!

If one spark in your bosom of virtue remains,
Go fan it with prayer till it kindles again;
Resolved, with "God helping," in future to be
From wine and its follies unshackled and free!
And when you have conquered
    this foe of your soul—
In manhood and honor beyond his control—
This heart will again beat responsive to thine,
And the lips free from liquor be welcome to mine.

Over the Hill to the Poor-House

By Will Carleton

Over the hill to the poor-house
   I'm trudgin' my weary way—
I, a woman of seventy, and only a trifle gray—
I, who am smart an' chipper,
   for all the years I've told,
As many another woman that's only half as old.

Over the hill to the poor-house—
   I can't quite make it clear!
Over the hill to the poor-house—
   It seems so horrid queer!
Many a step I've taken a-toilin' to and fro,
But this is a sort of journey I never thought to go.

What is the use of heapin'
   on me a pauper's shame?
Am I lazy or crazy? am I blind or lame?
True, I am not so supple, nor yet so awful stout;
But charity ain't no favor, if one can live without.

I am willin' and anxious an' ready any day
To work for a decent livin',
   an' pay my honest way;
For I can earn my victuals,
   an' more too, I'll be bound,
If anybody only is willin' to have me round.

Once I was young an' han'some—
   I was, upon my soul—
Once my cheeks was roses,
   my eyes as black as coal;

And I can't remember, in them days,
   of hearin' people say,
For any kind of reason, that I was in their way.

'T ain't no use of boastin', or talkin' over free,
But many a house an' home
   was open then to me;
Many a han'some offer I had from likely men,
An nobody ever hinted that I was a burden then.

And when to John I was married,
   sure he was good and smart,
But he and all the neighbors
   would own I done my part;
For life was all before me,
   an' I was young an' strong,
And I worked the best that I could
   in tryin' to get along.

And so we worked together:
   and life was hard, but gay,
With now and then a baby
   for to cheer us on our way;
Till we had half a dozen,
   an' all growed clean an' neat,
An' went to school like others,
   an' had enough to eat.

So we worked for the childr'n
   and raised 'em every one;
Worked for 'em summer and winter,
   just as we ought to've done;
Only perhaps we humored 'em,
   which some good folks condemn,
But every couple's child'rn's
   a heap the best to them.

Strange how much we think
   of our blessed little ones!—
I'd have died for my daughters,
   I'd have died for my sons!
And God he made that rule of love;
   but when we're old and gray,
I've noticed it sometimes, somehow fails
   to work the other way.

Strange, another thing;
  when our boys an' girls was grown,
And when, exceptin' Charley,
  they'd left us there alone;
When John he nearer an' nearer come,
  an' dearer seemed to be,
The Lord of Hosts he come one day
  and took him away from me.

Still I was bound to struggle,
  an' never to cringe or fall—
Still I worked for Charley,
  for Charley was now my all;
And Charley was pretty good to me,
  with scarce a word or frown,
Till at last he went a-courtin',
  and brought a wife from town.

She was somewhat dressy,
  an' hadn't a pleasant smile—
She was quite conceity, and
  carried a heap o' style:
But if ever I tried to be friends,
  I did with her, I know;
But she was hard and proud,
  an' I couldn't make it go.

She had an education,
  an' that was good for her,
But when she twitted me on mine,
  'twas carryin' things too fur,
An' I told her once, 'fore company
  (an' it almost made her sick),
That I never swallowed a grammar,
  or et a 'rithmetic.

So 'twas only a few days
  before the thing was done—
They was a family of themselves,
  and I another one;
And a very little cottage one family will do.
But I never have seen a house
  that was big enough for two.

An' I never could speak to suit her,
  never could please her eye.
An' it made me independent, an' then I didn't try;

But I was terribly staggered an' felt it like a blow,
When Charley turned ag'in me,
  an' told me I could go.

I went to live with Susan,
  but Susan's house was small,
And she was always a hintin'
  how snug it was for us all;
And what with her husband's sisters,
  and what with child'rn three,
'Twas easy to discover
  that there wasn't room for me.

An' then I went to Thomas,
  the oldest son I've got,
For Thomas' buildings'd cover the
  half of an acre lot;
But all the child'rn was on me—
  I couldn't stand their sauce—
And Thomas said I needn't think
  I was comin' there to boss.

An' then I wrote to Rebecca,
  my girl who lives out West,
And to Isaac, not far from her—
  twenty miles at best;
And one of 'em said 'twas too warm
  there for any one so old,
And t' other had an opinion
  the climate was too cold.

So they have shirked and slighted me,
  an' shifted me about—
So they have well-nigh soured me,
  an' wore my old heart out;
But still I've borne up pretty well,
  an' wasn't much put down,
Till Charley went to the poor-master,
  an' put me on the town.

Over the hill to the poor-house—
  my child'rn dear, good-by!
Many a night I've watched you
  when only God was nigh;
And God'll judge between us;
  but I will al'ays pray
That you shall never suffer the half I do today.

Over the Hill From the Poor-House

By Will Carleton

Editor's Note: *After "Over the Hill to the Poor-House" was first published in* Good Old Days *magazine, we received a letter from a reader from Will Carleton's home state of Michigan. The writer shared Carleton's sequel to "To the Poor-House," published in his* Farm Ballads *volume of verse.*

Carleton, being the kind and lovable man that he was, apparently was never satisfied to let that poor soul in his famous poem stay in the poor-house, so he wrote a sequel entitled "Over the Hill From the Poor-House." Many who have read the original poem, "Over the Hill to the Poor-House," are unaware of the sequel. To give a happy ending to the tale, here is the sequel. –K.T.

I, who was always counted, they say,
Rather a bad stick any way,
Splintered all over with dodges and tricks,
Known as "the worst of the Deacon's six";
I, the truant, saucy and bold,
The one black sheep in my father's fold,
"Once on a time," as the stories say,
Went over the hill on a winter's day—
Over the hill to the poor-house.

Tom could save what twenty could earn;
But givin' was somethin' he ne'er would learn;
Isaac could half o' the Scriptur's speak—
Committed a hundred verses a week;
Never forgot, an' never slipped;
But "Honor thy father and mother" he skipped;
So over the hill to the poor-house.

As for Susan, her heart was kind
An' good—what there was of it, mind;
Nothin' too big, and nothin' too nice,
Nothin' she wouldn't sacrifice
For one she loved; an' that 'ere one
Was herself, when all was said an' done.
And Charley an' 'Becca meant well, no doubt,
But any one could
   pull 'em about;

An' all o' our folks ranked well, you see,
Save one poor fellow, and that was me;
An' when one dark an' rainy night,
A neighbor's horse went out o' sight,
They hitched on me as the guilty chap
That carried one end o' the halter strap
An' I think, myself, that view of the case
Wasn't altogether out o' place;
My mother denied it, as mothers do,
But I am inclined to believe 'was true.
That I, as well as the horse, was led;
And the worst of whiskey spurred me on,
Or else the deed would never have been done.

But the keenest grief I ever felt,
Was when my mother beside me knelt,
An, cried an' prayed, till I melted down,
As I wouldn't for half the horses in town.
I kissed her fondly, then and there,
An' swore henceforth to be honest and square.

I served my sentence—a bitter pill
Some folks should take who never will;
And then I decided to go "out West,"
Concludin' 'twould suit my health the best;
Where, how I prospered, I never could tell,
But Fortune seemed to like me well,
An' somehow every vein I struck,
Was always bubblin' over with luck.
An' better than that, I was steady an' true,
An' put my good resolutions through.
But I wrote to a trusty old neighbor, an' said,
"You tell 'em, old fellow, that I am dead,
An' died a Christian; 'twill please 'em more,
Than if I had lived the same as before."

But when this neighbor he wrote to me,
"Your mother's in the poor-house," says he,
I had a resurrection straightaway,
An' started for her that very day.
An' when I arrived where I was grown,
I took good care that I shouldn't be known;
But I bought the old cottage, through and through,
Of someone Charley had sold it to;
And held back neither work nor gold,
To fix it up as it was of old,
The same big fire-place wide and high,
Flung up its cinders toward the sky;

The old clock ticked on the corner shelf—
I wound it an' set it agoin' myself;
An' if every thing wasn't the same,
Neither I nor money was to blame;
Then—
Over the hill to the poor-house!

One blowin', blusterin' winter's day,
With a team an' cutter I started away;
My fiery nags was as black as coal
(They some'at resembled the horse I stole);
I hitched an' entered the poor-house door—
A poor old woman was scrubbin' the floor;
She rose to her feet in great surprise,
And looked, quite startled, into my eyes;
I saw the whole of her trouble's trace
In the lines that marred her dear old face;
"Mother!" I shouted, "your sorrows is done!
You're adopted along o' your horse-thief son,
Come over the hill from the poor-house."

She didn't faint; she knelt by my side,
And thanked the Lord, till I fairly cried.
An' maybe our ride wasn't pleasant an' gay,
An' maybe she wasn't wrapped up that day;
An' maybe our cottage wasn't warm an' bright,
An' maybe it wasn't a pleasant sight,
To see her gettin' the evening tea,
An' frequently stoppin' and kissin' me;
An' maybe we didn't live happy for years,
In spite of my brothers' and sisters' sneers,
Who often said, as I have heard,
That they wouldn't own a prison bird;
(Though they're gettin' over that I guess,
For all of 'em owe me, more or less);

But I've learned one thing; an' it cheers a man
In always a-doin' the best he can;
That whether, on the big book, a blot
Gets over a fellow's name or not,
Whenever he does a deed that's white,
It's credited to him fair and right.
An' the Lord divides his sheep an' goats;
However they may settle my case,
Wherever they may fix my place,
My good old Christian mother, you'll see,
Will be sure to stand right up for me,
With over the hill from the poor-house.

The Year's at the Spring
By Robert Browning

The year's at the spring
And the day's at the morn;
Morning's at seven;
The hillside's dew-pearled;
The lark's on the wing;
The snail's on the thorn:
God's in His heaven ...
All's right with the world!

Woodman, Spare That Tree

By George P. Morris

Woodman, spare that tree!
Touch not a single bough!
In youth it sheltered me,
And I'll protect it now.
'Twas my forefather's hand
That placed it near his cot;
There, woodman let it stand
Thy ax shall harm it not!

That old familiar tree,
Whose glory and renown
Are spread o'er land and sea,
And would'st thou hew it down?
Woodman, forbear thy stroke!
Cut not its earth-bound ties!
Oh! spare that aged oak,
Now towering to the skies.

When but an idle boy,
I sought its grateful shade;
In all their gushing joy
Here too my sisters played.
My mother kissed me here
My father pressed my hand—
Forgive this foolish tear,
But let that old oak stand!

My heart-strings round thee cling
Close as thy bark, old friend!
Here shall the wild-bird sing,
And still thy branches bend.
Old tree, the storm still brave!
And, woodman, leave the spot!
While I've a hand to save,
Thy ax shall harm it not.

The Little White Dog *Author Unknown*

I remember years ago when I was rather small,
I used to go a-hunting
  with my brother in the fall.
If the air was still and frosty
  he would hardly ever miss,
Of an evening after supper to say, "Well, Sis
The work's all done, Old Dobb is right.
What say you if we take a trip tonight?
As I answered yes, I tried not to show
How glad I was that he'd asked me to go,
And tried to hide my pleasure and joy,
As being addressed as boy to boy.
I got my coat while brother took
The lantern down from the rusty hook.

And we started off at a leisurely jog
Followed closely by a little white dog.
He'd stay right by us until we came
To the wood at the end of a grassy lane.
Then brother would say, "Hist, hunt 'em up."
And we'd see no more of that little white pup
'Til some time later we'd hear him bark
Off to our right somewhere in the dark.
And I'd jump with
  delight and
  laugh with glee
While I
  wondered
  what he had
  in the
  tree.

Then brother would say, "Just cool off, Sue.
The little rascal ain't barking true.
No use to run until he growls;
There's nothing to those yelps and howls."
Again we'd sit upon the ground,
Our ears wide open to catch each sound.
Soon again we'd hear him bark
Off to our left somewhere in the dark.
And we could hear as it louder grew,
The growl wasn't there, again untrue.

Then brother would get his dander up.
And say, "Gol darn that little pup,
He ain't going to do no good, it appears;
Until I call him and pull his ears."
So he'd call him and pull them right,
And send him off again in the night.
And then as we sat upon the ground,
Our ears wide open to catch each sound,
It wasn't long 'til we heard his bark
Off to our right somewhere in the dark.
And brother would say, "Oh, hurry, Sue,
The good old rascal is barking true."
And sure enough when we came to the tree,
We found him true as true could be.
And for that night he proved sincere,
Because someone had pulled his ear.

'Tis years since then but I still can see
That little dog baying at an empty tree.
And I often think the people now
Are very much like that little bow-wow.
We follow each trail that fortune brings,
And like to worship empty things.
Like the little dog in days of old,
Who was changed from doubtful to true
  as gold,
We need a chastening, it appears,
Some friendly hand to pull our ears.

Old Shep *Author Unknown*

Now, when I was a lad and Old Shep was a pup,
Over hills and meadows, we'd stray.
Just a boy and his dog we were both full of fun;
We grew up together that way.

I remember the time at the old swimmin' hole;
When I would have drowned beyond doubt;
But Old Shep was right there—
   to the rescue he came—
He jumped in and helped pull me out.

The years fast did go—and at last he grew old;
His eyesight was fast growing dim.
And one day the doctor looked at me and said:
"I can't do no more for him, Jim."

With hands that were trembling,
   I picked up my gun—
I aimed it at Shep's faithful head

But I just couldn't do it; I wanted to run;
I wish they could shoot me instead.

He came to my side and he sat on the ground;
And lifted his old head to my knee;
And I stroked the best friend that a man ever had:
I cried so I scarcely could see.

Now Old Shep he knew he was going to go:
For he reached out and licked at my hand—
Then he looked up at me just as much as to say—
"We're parting"—but you understand.

Now Old Shep is gone,
   where the good doggies go—
And no more with Old Shep will I roam.
But it dogs have a heaven,
   there's one thing I know—
Old Shep has a wonderful home.

Out to Old Aunt Mary's

By James Whitcomb Riley

Wasn't it pleasant, O brother mine,
In those old days of the lost sunshine
Of youth—when the Saturday's chores were through,
And the "Sunday's wood" in the kitchen too,
And we were visiting, "me and you,"
Out to Old Aunt Mary's?—

"Me and you"—And the morning fair
With the dewdrops twinkling everywhere;
The scent of the cherry-blossoms blown
After us, in the roadway lone,
Our capering shadows onward thrown—
Out to Old Aunt Mary's!

It all comes back so clear to-day!
Though I am as bald as you are gray,—
Out by the barn-lot and down the lane
We patter along in the dust again,
As light as the tips of the drops of rain,
Out to Old Aunt Mary's.

The few last houses of the town;
Then on, up the high creek-bluffs and down;
Past the squat toll-gate, with its well-sweep pole,
The bridge, and "the old 'babtizin'-hole,'"
Loitering, awed, o'er pool and shoal,
Out to Old Aunt Mary's.

We cross the pasture, and through the wood,
Where the old gray snag of the poplar stood,
Where the hammering "red-heads" hopped awry,
And the buzzard "raised" in the "clearing"-sky
And lolled and circled, as we went by
Out to Old Aunt Mary's.

Or, stayed by the glint of the redbird's wings,
Or the glitter of song that the bluebird sings,
All hushed we feign to strike strange trails,
As the "big braves" do in the Indian tales,
Till again our real quest lags and fails—
Out to Old Aunt Mary's.—

And the woodland echoes with yells of mirth
That make old war-whoops of minor worth! …
Where such heroes of war as we?—
With bows and arrows of fantasy,
Chasing each other from tree to tree
Out to Old Aunt Mary's!

And then in the dust of the road again;
And the teams we met, and the countrymen;
And the long highway, with sunshine spread
As thick as butter on country bread,
Our cares behind, and our hearts ahead
Out to Old Aunt Mary's.—

For only, now, at the road's next bend
To the right we could make out the gable-end
Of the fine old Huston homestead—not
Half a mile from the sacred spot
Where dwelt our Saint in her simple cot—
Out to Old Aunt Mary's.

Why, I see her now in the open door
Where the little gourds grew up the sides and o'er
The clapboard roof!—And her face—ah, me!
Wasn't it good for a boy to see—
Wasn't it good for a boy to be
Out to Old Aunt Mary's?—

The jelly,—the jam and the marmalade,
And the cherry and quince "preserves" she made!
And the sweet-sour pickles of peach and pear,
With cinnamon in 'em, and all things rare!—
And the more we ate was the more to spare,
Out to Old Aunt Mary's!

Ah! was there, ever, so kind a face
And gentle as hers, or such a grace
Of welcoming, as she cut the cake
Or the juicy pies that she joyed to make
Just for the visiting children's sake—
Out to Old Aunt Mary's!

The honey, too, in its amber comb
One only finds in an old farm-home;
And the coffee, fragrant and sweet, and ho!
So hot that we gloried to drink it so,
With spangles of tears in our eyes, you know—
Out to Old Aunt Mary's.

And the romps we took, in our glad unrest!—
Was it the lawn we loved the best,
With its swooping swing in the locust trees,
Or was it the grove, with its leafy breeze,
Or the dim haymow, with its fragrancies—
Out to Old Aunt Mary's.

Continued …

Far fields, bottom-lands, creek-banks—all,
We ranged at will.—Where the waterfall
Laughed all the day as it slowly poured
Over the dam by the old mill-ford,
While the tail-race writhed, and the mill-wheel
  roared—
Out to Old Aunt Mary's.

But home, with Aunty in nearer call,
That was the best place, after all!—
The talks on the back porch, in the low
Slanting sun and the evening glow,
With the voice of counsel that touched us so,
Out to Old Aunt Mary's.

And then, in the garden—near the side
Where the beehives were and the path was wide,—
The apple-house—like a fairy cell—
With the little square door we knew so well,
And the wealth inside but our tongues could tell—
Out to Old Aunt Mary's.

And the old spring-house, in the cool green gloom
Of the willow trees,—and the cooler room
Where the swinging shelves and the crocks
  were kept,
Where the cream in golden languor slept,
While the waters gurgled and laughed and wept—
Out to Old Aunt Mary's.

And as many a time have you and I—
Barefoot boys in the days gone by—
Knelt, and in tremulous ecstasies
Dipped our lips into sweets like these,—
Memory now is on her knees
Out to Old Aunt Mary's.

For, O my brother so far away,
This is to tell you—she waits to-day
To welcome us: —Aunt Mary fell
Asleep this morning, whispering, "Tell
The boys to come." … And all is well
Out to Old Aunt Mary's.

It Couldn't Be Done

By Edgar A. Guest

Somebody said that it couldn't be done,
But he with a chuckle replied
That "maybe it couldn't," but he would be one
Who wouldn't say so 'til he'd tried.
So he buckled right in with the trace of a grin
On his face. If he worried he hid it.
He started to sing as he tackled the thing
That couldn't be done, and he did it.

Somebody scoffed: "Oh, you'll never do that;
At least no one ever has done it";
But he took off his coat and he took off his hat,
And the first thing we knew he'd begun it.
With a lift of his chin and a bit of a grin,
Without any doubting or quiddit,
He started to sing as he tackled the thing
That couldn't be done, and he did it.

There are thousands
  to tell you it
  cannot be done,
There are thousands
  to prophesy
  failure;
There are thousands
  to point out to
  you, one by one,
The dangers that wait
  to assail you.
But just buckle in with a
  bit of a grin,
Just take off your coat and go to it;
Just start to sing as you tackle
  the thing
That "cannot be done," and you'll do it.

Give the Flowers to the Living

By Will L. Thompson

Give the flowers to the living,
Let sweet fragrance fill the air;
Blessings follow with giving,
Pure and sweet as lily fair.

Give the toilers oft a token,
Of the love you would bestow;
Shower blessings on the living;
If you love them, tell them so.

Give the flowers to the living,
Give them honor, love and cheer;
Let them see appreciation
Of their labors while they're here.

Give encouragement and praises,
To the worthy ones you meet;
Sweetest blossoms for the living,
Strew the path for weary feet.

Give the flowers to the living,
Scatter blossoms on life's way;
You will see the glad thanksgiving,
Beaming heav'nward day by day.

Like the loving Magdalena,
Giving all she could bestow,
Shower blessings on the living;—
If you love them, tell them so.

Give me all the flowers today,
Whether pink or white or red;
I'd rather have one blossom now,
Than a truckload when I'm dead.

Christmas Selfishness

By E. Ellsworth Clasply

It was Christmas in a mansion;
There was gold and silver there,
Like queens of royal lineage,
The little ones did fare;
On rugs of silky velvet,
The children they were spread,
There were gifts of gold and ivory,
Costly toys where're you tread.

There were happy smiling faces,
There were sounds of joy and mirth,
Every wish fulfilled with good things,
All luxuries of the earth;
What a contrast to the manger,
Where the saintly Christ Child lay,
Where the shepherds they were guided,
By the star upon the way.

On this chill December evening
Came a rap upon the door,
A little tot with basket,
'Twas one of God's own poor,

The little face was haggard,
A rag about her head,
In a voice weak and trembling,
What she said was, "Gimme bread."

The lady dressed in satin
Gazed into her little face;
In her voice and in her manner
Of sympathy not a trace.
She replied, "We can't be bothered,
On this the Christmas night,"
As she closed the door quite snappy,
Shut the picture out of sight.

Next morning on the sidewalk,
Not very far away,
The little form lay frozen,
Hands clasped as though to pray.
The little one she slighted
Now sleeps beneath the sod,
Vengeance is mine, I will repay.
What will she say to God?

The First Snowfall

By James Russell Lowell

The snow had begun in the gloaming,
 And busily all the night
Had been heaping field and highway
 With a silence deep and white.

 Every pine and fir and hemlock
Wore ermine too dear for an earl,
And the poorest twig on the elm-tree
 Was ridged inch deep with pearl.

From sheds new-roofed with Carrara
 Came Chanticleer's muffled crow,
The stiff rails were softened to swan's-down,
 And still fluttered down the snow.

 I stood and watched by the window
 The noiseless work of the sky,
And the sudden flurries of snow-birds,
 Like brown leaves whirling by.

I thought of a mound in sweet Auburn
 Where a little headstone stood;
How the flakes were folding it gently,
 As did robins the babes in the wood.

 Up spoke our own little Mabel,
Saying, "Father, who makes it snow?"
 And I told of the good All-father
 Who cares for us here below.

 Again I looked at the snow-fall,
 And thought of the leaden sky
That arched o'er our first great sorrow,
 When that mound was heaped so high.

 I remembered the gradual patience
 That fell from that cloud-like snow,
 Flake by flake, healing and hiding
 The scar of our deep-plunged woe.

 And again to the child I whispered,
 "The snow that husheth all,
 Darling, the merciful Father
 Alone can make it fall!"

Then, with eyes that saw not, I kissed her;
 And she, kissing back, could not know
 That my kiss was given to her sister,
 Folded close under deepening snow.

The Passing of the Backhouse

By Charles T. Rankin

Editor's Note—For decades I have seen this poem published under the name of James Whitcomb Riley. Riley is one of my favorite poets, and I was confused by the attribution of "The Passing of the Backhouse" to him, for I had never found it published in any of the Riley anthologies. The poem was published many times under Riley's name in the pages of Good Old Days *magazine over the years before I became editor. Riley denied having written the poem and considered it risqué, but almost universally it was attributed to him. After much research, I discovered that another Hoosier, Charles T. Rankin, wrote the poem. A copy of the copyright is on display at the Fulton County Museum in Rochester, Ind. I hope this helps clear up the mystery of who truly was the author of "The Passing of the Backhouse" with all due apologies to Messrs. Riley and Rankin.—K.T.*

When memory keeps me
   company, and moves to smiles
   or tears,
A weather-beaten object looms
   through the mist of years;
Behind the house and barn it
   stood, a half a mile or more.
The hurrying feet a path had made,
   straight to the swinging door.
The architecture was a type of
   simple, classic art,
And in the tragedy of life it
   played a leading part.
And oft the passing traveler drove
   slow and heaved a sigh,
To see the modest hired girl slip
   out with glances shy.

We had our posy garden that the
   women loved so well.
I loved it too, but, better still, I
   loved the stronger smell
That filled the evening breezes so
   full of homely cheer,
And told the night-o'ertaken
   tramp that human life was near.
On lazy August afternoons it
   made a little bower
Delightful, where my grandsire
   sat and whiled away an hour,
For there the summer morning its
   very cares entwined,
And berry bushes reddened in the
   streaming soil behind.

All day fat spiders spun their
   webs to catch the buzzing flies
That flitted to and from the house,
   where Ma was baking pies.
And once a swarm of hornets bold
   had built a palace there,
And stung my unsuspecting aunt—
   I must not tell you where.
Then Father took a flaming
   pole—that was a happy day!
He nearly burned the building up,
   but the hornets left to stay.
When summer bloom began to
   fade, and winter to carouse,
We banked the little building with
   a heap of hemlock boughs.

But when the crust was on
   the snow and the sullen skies
   were gray,
In sooth, the building was no
   place where one could wish to
   stay.
We did our duties promptly—
   there one purpose swayed the
   mind.
We tarried not, nor lingered long
   on what we left behind.

The tortures of that icy seat could
   make a Spartan sob,
For needs must scrape the
   gooseflesh with a lacerating cob
That from a frost-encrusted nail
   was suspended by a string.
My father was a frugal man and
   wasted not a thing.

When Grandpa had to "go out
   back" and make his morning call,
We'd bundle up the dear old man
   with a muffler and a shawl.
I knew the hole on which he sat—
   'twas all too wide I found.
My loins were all too little, and I
   jackknifed there to stay
They had to come and get me out,
   or I'd have passed away.
Then Father said ambition was a
   thing that boys should shun,
And I must use the children's hole
   till childhood days were done.

But still I marvel at the craft that
   cut the holes so true;
The baby hole, and the slender
   hole that fitted sister Sue.
The dear old country landmark!
   I've traveled around a bit,
And in the lap of luxury has been
   my lot to sit.
But ere I die I'll eat the fruit of
   trees I robbed of yore,
Then seek the shanty where my
   name is carved above the door.
I ween the old, familiar smell will
   soothe my jaded soul,
I'm now a man—but nonetheless
   I'll try the baby hole.

A Hundred Years From Now

By Mary A. Ford

The surging sea of human life forever
  onward rolls,
And bears to the eternal shore its daily
  freight of souls;
Though bravely sails our bark today, pale
  Death sits at the prow,
And few shall know we ever lived a
  hundred years from now.

0 mighty human brotherhood! Why
  fiercely war and strive,
While God's great world has ample space
  for everything alive?
Broad fields uncultured and unclaimed
  are waiting for the plow
Of progress that shall make them bloom a
  hundred years from now.

Why should we try so earnestly in life's
  short, narrow span,
On golden stairs to climb so high above
  our brother man?
Why blindly at an earthly shrine in slavish
  homage bow?
Our gold will rust, ourselves be dust, a
  hundred years from now.

Why prize so much the world's applause?
  Why dread so much its blame?
A fleeting echo is its voice of censure or
  of fame;
The praise that thrills the heart, the scorn
  that dyes with shame the brow,
Will be as long-forgotten dreams a hundred
  years from now.

O patient hearts, that meekly bear your
  weary load of wrong,
O earnest hearts, that bravely dare, and
  striving, grow more strong!
Press on till perfect peace is won; you'll
  never dream of how
You struggled o'er life's thorny road a
  hundred years from now.

Grand, lofty souls, who live and toil that
  freedom, right and truth
Alone may rule the universe, for you is
  endless youth.
When 'mid the blest with God you rest, the
  grateful land shall bow
Above your clay in reverent love a
  hundred years from now.

Earth's empires rise and fall. Time! like
  breakers on thy shore
They rush upon thy rocks of doom, go
  down, and are no more.
The starry wilderness of worlds that gem
  night's radiant brow
Will light the skies for other eyes a
  hundred years from now.

Our Father, to whose sleepless eye the
  past and future stand
An open page, like babes we cling to Tby
  protecting hand;
Change, sorrow, death, are naught to us, if
  we may safely bow
Beneath the shadow of Thy throne a
  hundred years from now.

Memory and Grief

Chapter Four

Poetry has long been the voice of love and joy. Bards have long shared their musings of infatuation.

Still, the poetry from the Good Old Days had its memories laced with grief. The death of a child or a spouse was often the source of inspiration for a memorable poem or song.

How often my Grandma Stamps told me of "The Babes in the Wood" or of "The Letter Edged in Black." I still have "Grandfather's Clock" etched in my mind from singing it so many times with my mother when I was just a sprout.

Then there was "A Perfect Day." It was the theme song to a popular program back in the golden age of radio. I liked the music, but the words were what really entranced me. I had had some perfect days in my young life, and I knew the solitude and introspection Carrie Jacobs-Bond was trying to capture in the song. It was as if the end of a perfect day had a sad side—perhaps at the knowledge that the day was over and the long night awaited.

I memorized the words to the song and still am able to recite them by heart to this day. They remind me that even the best memories have a twinge of sadness to them. The poetry in this chapter, some of our mother's favorite verses, remind us of the close association of memory and grief.

—*Ken Tate*

A Perfect Day

By Carrie Jacobs-Bond

When you come to the end of a perfect day,
And you sit alone with your thought,
While the chimes ring out with a carol gay,
For the joy that the day has brought,
Do you think what the end of a perfect day
Can mean to a tired heart,
When the sun goes down with a flaming ray,
And the dear friends have to part?

Well this is the end of a perfect day,
Near the end of a journey, too;
But it leaves a thought that is big and strong,
With a wish that is kind and true.
For mem'ry has painted this perfect day
With colors that never fade,
And we find, at the end of a perfect day,
The soul of a friend we've made.

In the Baggage Coach Ahead

By Gussie L. Davis

On a dark stormy night, as the train rattled on,
All the passengers had gone to bed
Except one young man with a babe in his arms
Who sat there with bowed-down head.
The innocent one began crying just then,
As though its poor heart would break;
One angry man said, "Make that child stop
  its noise,
It's keeping all of us awake."
"Put it out," said another. "Don't keep it in here;
We've paid for our berths and want rest."
But never a word said the man with the child
As he fondled it close to his breast.

"Where is its mother? Go take it to her."
This a lady then softly said.
"I wish I could," was the man's sad reply,
"But she's dead in the coach up ahead."
Every eye filled with tears, when his story he told,
Of a wife who was faithful and true.
He told how he'd saved all his earnings for years,
Just to build up a home for two;

How, when Heaven had sent them this sweet
  little babe,
Their young happy lives were blessed.
His heart seemed to break when he mentioned
  her name,
And in tears tried to tell them the rest.
Ev'ry woman arose to assist with the child,
There were mothers and wives on that train,
And soon was the little one sleeping in peace
With no thought of sorrow or pain.
Next morning at a station, he bade all goodbye,
Each one had a story to tell in their home,
Of the baggage coach ahead.

While the train rolled onward,
A husband sat in tears,
Thinking of the happiness
Of just a few short years.
For baby's face brings pictures of
A cherished hope that's dead,
But baby's cries can't awaken her
In the baggage coach ahead.

A Package of Old Love Letters

Author Unknown

In a little rosewood casket,
Resting on a marble stand,
Is a package of old letters,
Written by a cherished hand,
Will you go and get them, Sister,
And read them all to me?
I have tried to do so often,
But for tears I could not see.

Come up near me, Dear Sister,
Let me lean upon your breast,
For the tide of life is ebbing,
And I soon shall be at rest.
Bring the letters he has written,
He whose words I've often heard.
Read them over, dear, distinctly,
For I have cherished every word.

Tell him, Sister, when you see him,
That I never ceased to love,
That I, dying, prayed to meet him,
In a better world above.
Tell me that I was supported,
Not a word of censure spoke,
But his silence and his absence,
This poor heart hath well-nigh broke.

Tell him I watched for his coming
When the noonday sun was high,
And when at evening the angels
Placed a starlight in the sky.
And when I saw he did not come,
Tell him that I did not chide,
But spoke in love about him,
And I blessed him as I died.

And when in death's white garments
You have wrapped my form around,
And have laid me down to slumber
In the quiet churchyard ground,
Place his letters and his picture
Close beside my pulseless heart.
We in life have been together,
And in death we will not part.

I am ready now, dear sister,
You may read the letter o'er,
And I'll listen to the words,
Of him who I shall see no more,
And when you have finished,
Should I calmly fall asleep,
Fall asleep in death and wake not,
Dearest sister, do not weep.

The Old Oaken Bucket

By Samuel Woodworth

How dear to my heart are the scenes of my
    childhood,
When fond recollection presents them to view!
The orchard, the meadow, the deep-tangled
    wildwood,
And every loved spot which my infancy
    knew,
The wide-spreading pond and the
    mill that stood by it,
The bridge and the rock where the
    cataract fell;
The cot of my father, the dairy
    house nigh it,
And e'en the rude-bucket which
    hung in the well.

The old oaken bucket,
    the iron-bound bucket,
The moss-covered bucket
    which hung in the well.

The moss-covered bucket I hail
    as a treasure;
From often at noon, when
    returned from the field,
I found it the source of an exquisite
    pleasure,
The purest and sweetest that nature
    can yield.
How ardent I seized it with hands that
    were glowing!
And quick to the white-pebbled bottom it fell;
Then soon, with the emblem of truth
    overflowing,
And dripping with coolness, it rose from the
    well.

The old oaken bucket,
    the iron-bound bucket,
The moss-covered bucket,
    it rose from the well.

How sweet from the green mossy brim to
    receive it,
As poised on the curb, it inclined to my lips!
Not a full blushing goblet could tempt me to
    leave it,

Though filled with the nectar that Jupiter sips.
And now, far removed from the loved situation,
The tear of regret will intrusively swell,
As fancy reverts to my father's plantation,
And sighs for the bucket that hung in the well.

The old oaken bucket,
    the iron-bound bucket,
The moss-covered bucket
    which hangs in the well.

The Babes in the Wood

Author Unknown

Now ponder well, you parents deare,
These wordes, which I shall write;
A doleful story you shall heare,
In time brought forth to light.
A gentleman of good
account
In Norfolke dwelt of late,
Who did in honour far surmount
Most men of his estate.

Sore sicke he was, and like to dye,
No helpe his life could save;
His wife by him as sicke did lye,
And both possest one grave.
No love between these two was lost,
Each was to other kinde;
In love they liv'd, in love they dyed,
And left two babes behinde:

The one a fine and pretty boy,
Not passing three yeares olde;
The other a girl more young than he,
And fram'd in beautyes molde.
The father left his little son,
As plainly doth appeare,
When he to perfect age should come,
Three hundred poundes a yeare.

And to his little daughter Jane
Five hundred poundes in gold,
To be paid downe on marriage-day,
Which might not be controll'd.
But if the children chance to dye,
Ere they to age should come,
Their uncle should possesse their wealth;
For so the wille did run.

"Now, brother," said the dying man,
"Look to my children deare;
Be good unto my boy and girl,
No friends else have they here:
To God and you I recommend
My children deare this daye;

But little while be sure we have
Within this world to staye."

"You must be father and mother both,
And uncle all in one;
God knowes what will become of them,
When I am dead and gone."
With that bespake their mother deare,
"O brother kinde," quote she,
"You are the man must bring our babes
To wealth or miserie:

"And if you keep them carefully,
Then God will you reward;
But if you otherwise should deal,
God will your deedes regard."
With lippes as cold as any stone
They kist their children small:
"God bless you both, my children deare";
With that the teares did fall.

These speeches then their brother spake
To this sicke couple there,
"The keeping of your little ones,
Sweet sister, do not feare;
God never prosper me nor mine,
Nor aught else that I have,
If I do wrong your children deare,
When you are layd in the grave."

The parents being dead and gone,
The children home he takes,
And bringes them straite into his house,
Where much of them he makes.
He had not kept these pretty babes
A twelvemonth and a daye,
But, for their wealth, he did devise
To make them bothe awaye.

He bargain'd with two ruffians strong,
Which were of furious mood,
That they should take these children young,
And slaye them in a wood.

He told his wife an artful tale,
He would the children send
To be brought up in faire London,
With one that was his friend.

Away then went these pretty babes,
Rejoycing at that tide,
Rejoycing with a merrye minde
They should on cock-horse ride.
They prate and prattle pleasantly,
As they rode on the waye,
To those that should their butchers be,
And work their lives' decaye:

So that the pretty speeche they had,
Made Murder's heart relent;
And they that undertooke the deed,
Full sore did now repent.
Yet one of them more hard of heart,
Did vowe to do his charge,
Because the wretch that hired him
Had paid him very large.

The other won't agree thereto,
So here they fall to strife;
With one another they did fight
About the children's life.
And he that was of mildest mood
Did slaye the other there,
Within an unfrequented wood—
The babes did quake for feare.

He took the children by the hand,
Teares standing in their eye,
And bade them straitwaye follow him,
And look they did not crye.
And two long miles he led them on,
While they for food complaine:
"Staye here," quoth he, "I'll bring you bread,
When I come backe againe."

These pretty babes, with hand in hand,
Went wandering up and downe;
But never more could see the man
Approaching from the town.
Their prettye lippes with black-berries
Were all besmear'd and dyed,
And when they saw the darksome night,
They sat them downe and cryed.

Thus wandered these poor innocents,
Till deathe did end their grief;
In one another's armes they dyed,
As wanting due relief.
No burial this pretty pair
Of any man receives,
Till Robin Redbreast piously
Did cover them with leaves.

And now the heavy wrath of God
Upon their uncle fell;
Yea, fearful fiends did haunt his house,
His conscience felt an hell;
His barnes were fir'd, his goodes consum'd
His landes were barren made,
His cattle dyed within the field,
And nothing with him stayed.

And in a voyage to Portugal
Two of his sons did dye;
And to conclude, himselfe was brought
To want and miserye.
He pawn'd and mortgag'd all his land
Ere seven yeares came about;
And now at length this wicked act
Did by this meanes come out:

The fellowe, that did take in hand
These children for to kill,
Was for a robbery judg'd to dye—
Such was God's blessed will:
Who did confess the very truth
As here hath been display'd:
Their uncle having dyed in gaol,
Where he for debt was layd.

You that executors be made,
And overseers eke
Of children that be fatherless,
And infants mild and meek;
Take you example by this thing,
And yield to each his right,
Lest God with such like miserye
Your wicked minds requite.

The Little Shirt That Mother Made for Me

Author Unknown

Now the first time I wore my
    knickerbocks,
It seemed so funny after wearing frocks,
I looked a little picture, so they say,
And then they sent me out to run and play,
But I didn't like the trousers
    I was wearing,
So, in the street I took them off, you see,
And started marching off
    so brave and daring
In that little shirt my Mother made for me.

And then, to school they said that I
    must go,
Even like my teacher, you must know,
So when I played the truant quite so dear,
The teacher said, "Bradley, you come here."
With a big stick she beat around on me,
There's no mistake about my pedigree,
I had the map of Scotland printed on me
'Neath the little shirt my Mother made
    for me.

I'll never forget the day that I was born,
It was on a cold and frosty Winter's morn
When the nurse, she took me on her lap
And said I was a chubby little chap.
Then they took me
    and washed me all over,
And then they powder-puffed me,
    and don't you see,
Then they laid me in the cradle
    by the fireside
In that little shirt my Mother made for me.

Last year when on my holiday
Upon the briny ocean I did gaze,
The water looked so fine I thought I'd go
To have a swim, but in a minute, Oh!
All the girls on the beach
    at me were staring
And some were taking pictures,
    I could see
'Twas very good for me
    that I was wearing
That little shirt my Mother made for me.

The Letter Edged in Black

Author Unknown

I was standing by my window
    yesterday morning,
Without a thought of worry or care
When I saw the postman
    coming down the pathway
With such a happy smile and a jaunty air.
O, he rang the bell, and whistled
    while he waited,
And then he said,
    "Good morning to you, Jack";
But he little knew the sorrow
    that he brought me,
When he handed me
    a letter edged in black.

Chorus:
As I heard the postman whistling
    yesterday morning,
Coming down the pathway with his pack,
O, he little knew the sorrow
    that he brought me
When he handed me
    a letter edged in black.

Then with trembling hands I took the
    letter from him,
I broke the seal and this is what it said:
"Come home, my boy, your poor old
    father wants you,
Come home, my boy,
    your mother dear is dead.
O, your mother's words,
    the last she uttered,
Were, 'Tell my boy I want him
    to come back.'
My eyes are blurred,
    my poor old heart is breaking,
While I'm writing you
    this letter edged in black."

O, I bow my head in sadness
    and in sorrow,
The sunlight of my life it now has fled,
Since the postman brought
    that letter yestermorning,
Saying, "Come home, my boy,
    your dear mother's dead."
O, it said, "Forgive the angry words
    t'were spoken,
You know I never meant them,
    don't you, Jack?
O, the angels bear me witness,
    I am asking
Your forgiveness in
    this letter edged in black."

The Tie That Binds

By Charles K. Harris

Within a small room, cold and cheerless,
There sits a young woman alone,
Beside her a cradle stands empty,
While o'er it she sobs and moans,
"My husband, he no longer loves me,
His love vanished when baby died,
So I'll leave him and our home forever,
And out in the cold world abide."

She packs baby's clothes in a bundle,
While tears slowly flow down her cheeks,
"I never would leave him, no, never,
If only one kind word he'd speak."
Just then the door quickly is opened,
Her husband takes the bundle away,
And he spreads the things out on the table,
While, gently to her he does say:

Chorus:
One little stocking for you, Nell,
One tiny blue shoe for me,
One baby's wrap and small lace cap,
We'll share in memory.
One lock of hair is for you, dear,
See how the golden curl shines,
And we'll both keep her smile as she sleeps,
For she's the tie that binds.

In silence they gaze at each other,
Then softly his darling wife said:
"Today is our third anniversary,
Just three years ago we wed;
Remember the seat in the orchard,
Where we would meet day after day,
And 'twas there with your arms close about me
You called me your queen of May."

"And don't you remember the parson!"
He cried with his face all aglow,
"I hear his voice saying, 'God bless you!
You'll be a good man to her, Joe.'"
Then closer they draw to each other,
"Ah darling," he said, "won't you stay,
If it's only in memory of baby,
I promise I'll never more say:

Chorus:
One little stocking for you, Nell,
One tiny blue shoe for me,
One baby's wrap and small lace cap,
We'll share in memory.
One lock of hair is for you, dear,
See how the golden curl shines,
And we'll both keep her smile as she sleeps,
For she's the tie that binds."

Grandfather's Clock

By Henry Clay Work

My grandfather's clock was too large for the shelf,
So it stood ninety years on the floor;
It was taller by half than the old man himself,
    though it weighed not a pennyweight more.
It was bought on the morn of the day that he
    was born,
And was always his treasure and pride.
But it stopp'd short never to go again
When the old man died.

Ninety years, without slumbering,
Tick, tock, tick, tock!
His life seconds numbering
Tick, tock, tick, tock!
It stopp'd short never to go again,
When the old man died.

In watching its pendulum swing to and fro,
Many hours had he spent while a boy;
And in childhood and manhood
    the clock seemed to know,
And to share both his grief and his joy.
For it struck twenty-four
    when he enter'd at the door,
With a blooming and beautiful bride.
But it stopp'd short never to go again,
When the old man died.

Ninety years, without slumbering,
Tick, tock, tick, tock!
His life seconds numbering
Tick, tock, tick, tock!
It stopp'd short never to go again,
When the old man died.

My grandfather said of those he could hire,
Not a servant so faithful he found
For it wasted no time and had but one desire—
At the close of each week to be wound.
And it kept in its place—not a frown on its face,
And its hands never hung by his side;
But it stopp'd short never to go again,
When the old man died.

Ninety years, without slumbering,
Tick, tock, tick, tock!

His life seconds numbering
Tick, tock, tick, tock!
It stopp'd short never to go again,
When the old man died.

It rang an alarm in the dead of the night;
An alarm that for years had been dumb.
And we knew that his spirit was pluming
    for flight,
That his hour for departure had come
Still the clock kept the time
    with a soft muffled chime
As we silently stood by his side;
But it stopp'd short never to go again,
When the old man died.

Ninety years, without slumbering,
Tick, tock, tick, tock!
His life seconds numbering
Tick, tock, tick, tock!
It stopp'd short never to go again,
When the old man died.

Casey Jones

By Wallace Saunders

Editor's Note: *This popular vaudeville song version of the original "Ballad of Casey Jones" was published in the November 1910* The Railroad Man's Magazine.—*K.T.*

Come all you rounders if you want to hear
The story of a brave engineer;
Casey Jones was the rounder's name,
And on a six-eight wheeler did he win his fame.

Caller called Casey at a half past four,
He kissed his wife at the station door,
Mounted to the cab with his orders in his hand,
And took his farewell trip to the promised land.

Through South Memphis yards on the fly,
He heard the fore boy say,
   "You've got a white eye."
All the switchmen knew by the engine's moans
That the man at the throttle was Casey Jones.

It had been raining some five or six weeks,
The railroad track was like the bed of a creek.
They rated him down to a thirty-mile gait,
Threw the southbound mail about eight hours late.

Fireman says, "Casey, you're running too fast,
You run the block board
   the last station you passed."
Jones says, "Yes, I believe we'll make it, though.
For she steams better than I ever knew."

"So pour in the water,
And shovel in the coal,
Stick your head out the window,
And watch them drivers roll."

Jones says, "Fireman, don't you fret;
Keep knockin' at the fire door, don't give up yet.
I'm going to run her till she leaves the rail,
Or make it on time with the Southern mail."

Around the curve and down the dump,
Two locomotives were bound to bump.
Fireman hollered, "Jones, it's just ahead,
We might jump and make it, but we'll all be dead."

'Twas around this curve he spied
   a passenger train,
Rousing his engine he caused the bell to ring;
Fireman jumped off, but Casey stayed on—
He's a good engineer, but he's dead and gone.

Casey said just before he died,
"There's two more roads that I'd like to ride."
The fireman said, "What can they be?"
"The Southern Pacific and the Santa Fe."

Poor Casey Jones was all right,
For he stuck to his duty both day and night,
They loved to hear his whistle
   and the ring of number three,
As he came into Memphis on the old I.C.

Mrs. Jones sat on the bed a-crying;
Just received the message that Casey was dying—
Says, "Go to bed, children, and hush you cryin',
Cause you got another papa on the Salt Lake Line."

Headaches and heartaches and all kinds of pain
Are not apart from a railroad train;
Tales that are in earnest, noble and grand,
Belong to the life of a railroad man.

The Wreck of Number Nine

Author Unknown

On a cold, winter night,
Not a star was in sight
And the north wind was howling down the line;
With his sweetheart so dear
Stood a brave engineer,
With his orders to pull old Number Nine.

She kissed him good-bye
With a tear in her eye,
But the joy in his heart he could not hide,
For the whole world was bright
When she told him that night
That tomorrow she'd be his blushing bride.

Oh, the wheels hummed a song
As the train rolled along
And the black smoke came pouring from the stack,
And the headlights agleam
Seemed to brighten his dream
Of tomorrow, when he'd be going back.

He sped 'round the hill
And his brave heart stood still,
For a headlight was shining in his face;
Then he whispered a prayer
As he threw on the air,
For he knew this would be his final race.

In the wreck he was found
Lying there on the ground,
And he asked them to raise his weary head;
As his breath slowly went,
This message he sent
To the maiden who thought she would be wed:

"There's a little white home
That I bought for our own,
Where I dreamed we'd be happy by-and-by,
And I leave it to you,
For I know you'll be true,
Till we meet at the Golden Gate—Good-bye."

The Wreck of the Old 97

Author Unknown

Well, they gave him his orders
   at Monroe, Virginia
Sayin', "Steve, you're way behind time.
This is not Thirty-Eight; it is old Ninety-Seven.
You must put her into Spencer on time."

Then he turned and said
   to his black greasy fireman
"Hey, shovel in a little more coal
For when we cross that White Oak Mountain
Watch old Ninety-Seven roll."

It's a mighty rough road
   from Lynchburg to Danville
With a line on a three-mile grade;
It was on that grade that he lost his airbrakes
And you see what a jump he made.

He was going down the grade
   makin' ninety miles an hour
When his whistle broke into a scream!
He was found in the wreck,
   with his hand on the throttle,
Scalded to death by the steam.

The telegram came from the Washington station
This is how it read:
"Oh that brave engineer that run old Ninety-Seven
Is lying in old Danville, dead!"

So now all you ladies better take fair warnin'
From this time on and learn.
Never speak harsh words
   to your true lovin' husband
He may leave you and never return!

Bed-time *By Annie B. Stephens*

Mother Night has drawn her curtain,
   Called her wee ones all to rest,
Small feet pattering, small tongues chattering,
   Seeking each its snowy nest.

Button that won't be unbuttoned—
   Tied up tight one willful shoe—
Tiny fingers tired of trying—
   "Tuzzin Annie, wha' sall I do?"

Little face so sad and sober,
   "Tuzzin Annie, my feets is told!"
Tears that can't help running over,
   His patience is but three years old.

In my arms I fold him closely,
   Dry his tears and soothe his woes,
Then before the friendly fireplace
   Toast his tired little toes.

Perched up in her chair beside me,
   Little woman, six years old,
Night makes her once more a baby—
   In each hand two feet I hold.

"Tell us, please, two little stories,
   One for baby, one for me,
First about the three gray squirrels
   High up in the button-ball tree."

This one told, she begs another,
   "Nothing more to-night, my dear;"
But the "no" that ends a story
   Hardest is for her to hear.

Baby boy in comfort resting,
   Cares no more his eyes to close,
Watching how the red light flashes
   Through the grating of his toes.

Into bed I closely tuck them,
   Kiss their lips and smooth their hair,
Fold their hands and watch beside them
   While they say their evening prayer.

Praying with them to "Our Father,"
   "Through this night the children keep
Who o'er all the earth are lisping
   'Now I lay me down to sleep.'"

Bury Me Not on the Lone Prairie

Author Unknown

"Oh bury me not on the lone prairie!"
These words came low and mournfully
From the pallid lips of a youth who lay
On his dying bed at the close of day.

He had waited and pined till o'er his brow
Death's shadows fast were drawing now,
He had thought of home and the loved ones nigh,
As the cowboys gathered to see him die.

How oft I've heard the well-known words
Of the wild winds and the sounds of birds.
I've thought of home and the cottage in a bower,
Of the scenes I loved in that childhood hour.

I've always wished to be laid when I died
In the churchyard on the green hillside;
By my father's grave, there let mine be,
And bury me not on the lone prairie.

And there is another whose tears will be shed
For one who lies on a prairie bed;
It pained me then and it pains me now—
She has curled these locks,
    she has kissed this brow.

"Oh, bury me not," and his voice failed there;
But we took no heed of his dying prayer.
In a narrow grave just six by three,
We laid him there on the lone prairie.

Where the dewdrops fall and the butterfly rests,
The wild rose blooms on the prairie's crest;
Where the coyotes howl and the wind sports free,
We laid him there on the lone prairie.

Bury Me Not on the Lone Prairie

Auther Unknown
Version 2

"Oh bury me not on the lone prairie!"
These words came low and mournfully
From the pallid lips of a youth who lay
On his dying bed at the close of day.

"O bury me not on the lone prairie,
Where the wild coyotes will howl o'er me,
Where the buzzards beat
    and the wind goes free;
O bury me not on the lone prairie!

"O bury me not on the lone prairie,
In a narrow grave six foot by three,
Where the buffalo paws o'er a prairie sea;
O bury me not on the lone prairie!

"O bury me not on the lone prairie,
Where the wild coyotes will howl o'er me,
Where the rattlesnakes hiss
    and the crow flies free;
O bury me not on the lone prairie!

"Oh, bury me not," and his voice faltered there,
But we took no heed of his dying prayer;
In a narrow grave just six by three,
We laid him there on the lone prairie.

Little Brown Hands *Author Unknown*

They drive home the cows from the pasture,
Up through the long, shady lane,
Where the quail whistles loud in the wheat fields
That are yellow with ripening grain.
They find in the thick, weaving grasses,
Where the scarlet-lipped strawberries grow;
They gather the earliest snow drops,
And the first crimson bud of the rose.

They toss the new hay in the meadow;
They gather the elder-blooms white;
They find where dusky grapes purple,
In the soft-tinted October light.
They know where the apples hang ripest,
And are sweeter than Italy's wines;
They know where the fruit hangs thickest,
On the long, thorny blackberry vines.

They gather the delicate seaweeds,
And build tiny castles of sand
They pick the beautiful seashells—
Fairy barks that have drifted to land,
They wave from the tall, rocking treetops,
Where the oriole's hammock-nest swings;
And at nighttime are folded in slumber
By a song that a fond mother sings.

They who toil bravely are strongest;
The humble and poor become great,
And so from these brown-handed children
Shall grow mighty rulers of state.
The pen of the author and statesman—
The noble and wise of the land—
The sword, and the chisel, and palette,
Shall be held in the little brown hand.

John Slobodnik

Two Little Stockings

Author Unknown

Two little stockings hung side by side
Close to the fireplace broad and wide.
"Two?" said St. Nick as down he came
Loaded with toys and many a game.

"Oh ho!" said he with a laugh of fun,
"I'll have no cheating my pretty one,
I know who lives in this house, my dear,
There's only one little girl lives here."

So he crept up close to the chimney place
And measured a sock with a sober face;
Just then a wee little note fell out
And fluttered low, like a bird about.
"Ah, Ha! What's this?" said he in surprise,
As he pushed his specs up close to his eyes
And read the address in a child-like hand;

"Dear St. Nicholas," so it began,
"The other stocking you see on the wall
I have hung for a child named Clara Hall.
She's a poor little girl, but very good,
So I thought perhaps you kindly would
Fill up her stocking, too, tonight
And help to make her Christmas bright,
If you've not enough for both stockings there,
Please put all in Clara's, I shall not care."

St. Nicholas brushed a tear from his eye
And, "God bless you, darling,"
   he said with a sigh.
Then softly he blew through the chimney high
A note like a bird's as it soared on high,
When down came two of the funniest mortals
That ever were seen this side of earth's portals.
"Hurry up," said St. Nick, "and nicely prepare
All a little girl needs where money is rare."

Then oh, what a scene there was in that room;
Away went the elves, but down from the gloom
Of the sooty old chimney comes tumbling low
A child's full wardrobe from head to toe.
How Santa laughed as he gathered them in,
And fastened each one to the sock with a pin.
Right to the toe he hung a blue dress,
"She'll think it came from the sky,"
Said St. Nicholas, smoothing the folds of blue,
And tying a hood to the stocking, too.

When all the warm clothes were fastened on,
And both little socks were filled and done,
Then Santa Claus tucked a toy here and there
And hurried away through the frosty air.
Saying, "God pity the poor,
   and bless the dear child
Who pities them too on a night so wild."

The wind caught the words
   and bore them on high
Till they died away in the midnight sky,
While St. Nicholas flew through the icy air,
Bringing "peace and good will"
   with him everywhere.

The Children's Hour

By Henry Wadsworth Longfellow

Between the dark and the daylight,
When the light is beginning to lower,
Comes a pause in the day's occupations,
That is known as the Children's Hour.

I hear in the chamber above me
The patter of little feet,
The sound of a door that is opened,
And voices soft and sweet.

From my study I see in the lamplight,
Descending the broad hall stair,
Grave Alice and laughing Allegra,
And Edith with golden hair.

A whisper, and then a silence;
Yet I know by their merry eyes,
They are plotting and planning together
To take me by surprise.

A sudden rush from the stairway,
A sudden raid from the hall!
By three doors left unguarded
They enter my castle wall!

They climb up into my turret,
O'er the arms and back of my chair;
If I try to escape, they surround me;
They seem to be everywhere.

They almost devour me with kisses,
Their arms about me entwine,
Till I think of the Bishop of Bingen
In his Mouse-Tower on the Rhine.

Do you think, O blue-eyed banditti,
Because you have scaled the wall,
Such an old mustache as I am
Is not a match for you all?

I have you fast in my fortress,
And will not let you depart,
But put you down in the dungeon
In the round-tower of my heart.

And there will I keep you forever,
Yes, forever and a day,
Till the walls shall crumble to ruin,
And moulder in dust away.

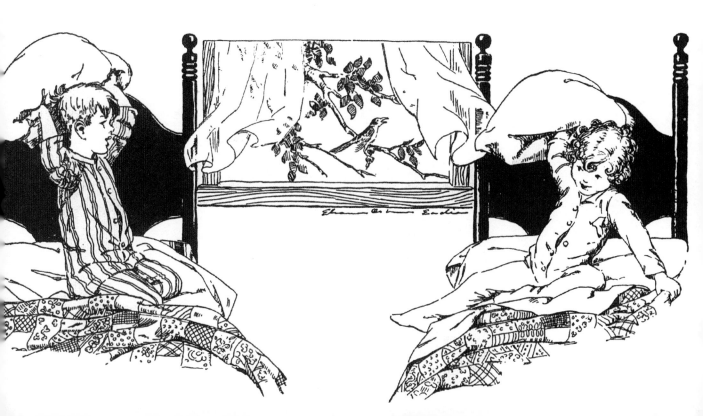

The Christmas Sleigh Ride

By Helen Gray Cone

They started from the old farm-gate,
The happiest boys alive,
With Rob, the roan, and Rust, his mate,
And Uncle Jack to drive;
The snow was packed, that Christmas-time,
The moon was round and clear,
And when the bells began to chime,
They all began to cheer.
Chime, chime, chime, chime,—such a merry load
Sleighing in the moonlight along the river road!

They passed the lonely cider mill,
That's falling all apart;
The hermit heard them on the hill,—
It warmed his frozen heart;
They cheered at every farmhouse gray,
With window-panes aglow,—
Within, the farmer's wife would say,
"Well, well, I want to know!"
Chime, chime, chime, chime,—such a noisy load
Speeding by the homesteads along the river road!

The river shone, an icy sheet,
As o'er the bridge they flew;
Then down the quiet village street
Their Christmas horns they blew;
The sober people smiled and said,
"We'll have to give them leave
(Boys will be boys!) to make a noise,
Because it's Christmas-Eve!"
Chime, chime, chime, chime,—such a lively load
Scattering songs and laughter along the river road!

But now it's growing hard to keep
Awake, and now it seems
The very bells have gone to sleep,
And jingle in their dreams.
The lane at last,—the farm-gate creaks,
And Grandma cries, "It's Jack!
Why, what a peck of apple-cheeks
These boys have brought us back!"
Chime, chime, chime, chime,—such a hungry load,
Rosy from the Christmas ride along the river road!

Love & Friendship

Chapter Five

*I*f poetry incites memories of grief, it gives equal time to love and friendship. In our courting days, I often penned Janice lines extolling my great love for her. I know she kept those lines in her keepsakes, but I'm thankful she doesn't get them out too often. A great poet I am not.

No, it was easier for me to pull out a copy of Elizabeth Barrett Browning's *Sonnets of the Portuguese* and recite her "Sonnet #43." That always brought a blush to Janice's cheeks and caused her heart to race just a little.

The poems and songs in this chapter will take you back to a time of innocence. It will remind you of the days when a boy wouldn't be embarrassed to read his best girl a few verses in hopes of winning her heart—and hand.

Settle in for a sentimental journey—and be sure to take a parasol—as we remember mother's favorite verses of love and friendship.

—*Ken Tate*

Sonnet #43
How Do I Love Thee?

By Elizabeth Barrett Browning

How do I love thee? Let me count the ways.
I love thee to the depth and breadth and height
My soul can reach, when feeling out of sight
For the ends of Being and ideal Grace.
I love thee to the level of every day's
Most quiet need, by sun and candlelight.
I love thee freely, as men strive for Right:
I love thee purely, as they turn from Praise.
I love thee with the passion put to use
In my old griefs, and with my childhood's faith.
I love thee with a love I seemed to lose
With my lost saints,—I love thee with the breath,
Smiles, tears, of all my life!—and, if God choose,
I shall but love thee better after death.

In Lilac Time

Author Unknown

The bobolink sung to 'is mate,
The doves wuz softly cooin',
I heard the clinkin' of the gate,
When Joe first come a-wooin'.

I stood beside the lilock bush
(The sun was slowly sinkin');
My cheeks was all to once a-blush,
When I heard the gate-latch clinkin'.

Fer Joe he wuz so good an' kind
(Tho' such a bashful lover),
No truer friend you'd ever find
In all the wide world over.

He sez, "Ez I wuz goin' by,
I seed yer hair so shiny,
Yer eyes ez blue ez summer sky,
Yer cheeks ez red's a piny;

"My heart my throat come thrummin' in,
The dusk it struck my fancy;
I couldn't help a-comin' in
An' speakin' to ye, Nancy."

An' then —'e sez—O me!
My feelins gits unruly—
He'd liked me all along, you see;
I know he loved me truly.

An' I wuz but an orphan, too,
A-workin' fer my livin',
Without a kith er kin I knew,
An' jest myself to give 'im.

An' when 'iz voice sunk soft away—
A kind o' tremblin' in it—
The words I tried so hard to say
Kep' chokin' fer a minute.

The lilock blossoms wuz in blow,
So sweet, with dewdrops beaded;
I handed 'im a bunch, an' Joe
No other answer needed.

The year it passed, the war wuz come,
The soldiers fast enrollin';
I heard the beatin' of the drum,
I thought like church-bell tollin'.

I stood beside the lilock bush,
The shadows round me lyin',
An' all the evenin' in a hush,
Except the wind a-sighin';

An' down the lane the whip-'oor-will
So sad an' mournful callin'—
Somehow it wuz so dreadful still,
The tears would keep a-fallin'.

An' then he come—so brave an' strong,
An' yet 'is lips a-quiv'rin';
I guesst 'is errant all along,
An' couldn't help a-shiv'rin'.

O friend, the year went round—went round—
But this'll tell you better;
This withered lilock someone found,
An' sent me in a letter.

Ah, well! there's more than me that know
How sad is war, an' fearful,
An' since the good God plans it so,
I must try to be cheerful;

But when the lilocks air in bloom,
An' when the day's a-dyin',
I creep off to my little room
An' have a fit of cryin'.

Should You Go First

Author Unknown

Should you go first and I remain
To walk the road alone,
I'll live in memory's garden, dear,
With happy days we have known.
In Spring I'll wait for the roses red,
When fades the lilac blue;
In early Fall when brown leaves call,
I'll catch a glimpse of you.

Should you go first and I remain
To finish with the scroll,
No lengthening shadows
shall creep in
To make this life seem droll.
We've known so much
happiness,
We've known our cup of joy,
And memory is one gift of God
That death can not destroy.

Should you go first
and I remain
For battles to be fought,
Each thing you have touched
along the way
Will be a hallowed spot.
I'll hear your voice,
I'll see your smile,
Though blindly I may grope,
The memory of your helping hand
Will buoy me on with hope.

Should you go first and I remain,
One thing I'd have you do:
Walk slowly down the path of death,
For one day I'll follow you.
I'll want to know each step you take,
That I may walk the same.
For some day down that lonely road,
You'll hear me call your name.

Silver Threads Among the Gold

Author Unknown

Darling, I am growing old.
Silver threads among the gold
Shine upon my brow today,
Life is fading fast away;
But, my darling, you will be
Always young and fair to me.

When your hair is silver white
And your cheeks no longer bright
With the roses of the May,
I will kiss your lips and say:
"Oh, my darling, mine alone, alone,
You have never older grown."

Love can never more grow old,
Locks may lose their brown and gold,
Cheeks may fade and hollow grow,
But the hearts that love will know
Never, never winter's frost and chill;
Summer warmth is in them still.

Love is always young and fair;
What to me is silver hair,
Faded cheeks or step grown slow
To the heart that beats below?
Since I kissed you mine alone, alone,
You have never older grown.

Maple on the Hill

Author Unknown

Near a quiet country village,
  stood a maple on the hill
Where I sat with Jeanetta long ago,
When the stars were slowly peeping,
And we heard the whip-poor-wills.
There we vowed to love each other
  evermore.

We would sing love songs together
  when the birds had gone to rest,
And would listen to the murmur
  of the rill.

Then I'd close my arms around her,
Lay my head upon her breast
When we sat beneath the maple
  on the hill.

We are getting old and feeble,
  yet the stars are shining bright.
And we listen to the murmur
  of the rill.
Will you always love me darling,
As you did on starry nights,
When we sat beneath the maple
  on the hill?

Don't forget me, little darling,
  when they lay me down to rest
Place a little bunch of flowers,
  grant I crave
When you linger there in sadness
Thinking darling of the past.
Let your teardrops kiss the flowers
  on my grave.

I will soon be with the angels
  on that bright and peaceful shore.
Even now I hear them coming
  o'er the hill.
Oh good-bye, my little darling,
For my time has come.
You and I must part,
I must leave you and the maple
  on the hill.

Love at Home

Author Unknown

There is beauty all around,
When there's love at home;
There is joy in every sound,
When, there's love at home.
Peace and plenty here abide,
Smiling sweet on every side,
Time doth softly, sweetly glide,
When there's love at home.

Love at home, Love at home,
Time doth softly, sweetly glide,
When, there's love at home.

In the cottage there is joy,
When, there's love at home;
Hate and envy ne'er annoy,
When, there's love at home;
Roses blossom 'neath our feet,
All the earth's a garden sweet;
Making life a bliss complete,
When there's love at home.

Love at home, Love at home,
Making life a bliss complete,
When there's love at home.

Kindly heaven smiles
    above,
When there's love
    at home;
All the earth is filled
    with love,
When there's love
    at home.
Sweeter sings the
    brooklet by,
Brighter beams
    the azure sky,
Oh, there's one who smiles
    on high,
When there's love at home.

Love at home, Love at home,
Oh, there's one who smiles above,
When there's love at home.

Jesus, show Thy mercy mine,
Then there's love at home;
Sweetly whisper I am Thine,
Then there's love at home.
Source of love, Thy cheering light,
Far exceeds the sun so bright,
Can dispel the gloom of night,
Then there's love at home.

Love at home, Love at home,
Can dispel the gloom of night,
When there's love at home.

Betsy and I Are Out

By Will Carleton

Draw up the papers, lawyer,
    and make 'em good and stout;
For things at home are crossways,
    and Betsy and I are out.
We, who have worked together
    so long as man and wife,
Must pull in single harness
    for the rest of our nat'ral life.

"What is the matter?" say you.
    I swear it's hard to tell!
Most of the years behind us
    we've passed by very well;
I have no other woman,
    she has no other man—
Only we've lived together
    as long as we ever can.

So I have talked with Betsy,
    and Betsy has talked with me,
An we've agreed together
    that we can't ever agree;
Not that we've catched each other
    in any terrible crime;
We've been a-gathering this for years,
    a little at a time.

There was a stock of temper
    we both had for a start,
Altho we never suspected
    'twould take us two apart;
I had my various failings,
    bred in the flesh and bone;
And Betsy, like all good women,
    had a temper of her own.

The first thing I remember
    whereon we disagreed
Was something concerning heaven—
    a difference in our creed;
We arg'ed the thing at breakfast,
    we arg'ed the thing at tea.
And the more we arg'ed the question
    the more we didn't agree.

And the next that I remember
    was when we lost a cow;
She had kicked the bucket for certain,
    the question was only—How?

I held my own opinion,
    and Betsy another had;
And when we were done a-talkin',
    we both of us were mad.

And the next that I remember,
    it started in a joke;
But full for a week it lasted,
    and neither of us spoke.
And the next was when I scolded
    because she broke a bowl,
And she said I was mean and stingy,
    and hadn't any soul.

And so that bowl kept pourin'
    dissensions in our cup;
And so that blamed cow-critter
    was always a-comin' up;
And so that heaven we arg'ed
    no nearer to us got,
But it gave us a taste of somethin'
    a thousand times as hot.

And so the thing kept workin'
    and all the self-safe way;
Always somethin' to arg'e
    and somethin' sharp to say;
And down on us came the neighbors,
    a couple dozen strong,
And lent their kindest sarvice
    for to help the thing along.

And there has been days together—
    and many a weary week—
We was both of us cross and spunky,
    and both too proud to speak;
And I have been thinkin' and thinkin',
    the whole of the winter and fall,
If I can't live kind with a woman,
    why then, I won't at all.

And so I have talked with Betsy,
    and Betsy has talked with me,
And we have agreed together
    that we can't never agree;
And what is hers shall be hers,
    and what is mine shall be mine;
And I'll put it in the agreement,
    and take it to her to sign.

Write on the paper lawyer—
    the very first paragraph—
Of all the farm and livestock
    that she shall have her half;
For she has helped to earn it,
    through many a weary day,
And it's nothing more than justice
    that Betsy has her pay.

Give her the house and homestead—
    a man can thrive and roam;
But women are skeery critters,
    unless they have a home;
And I have always determined,
    and never failed to say,
That Betsy never should want a home
    if I was taken away.

There is a little hard money
    that's drawin' tol'rable pay;
A couple of hundred dollars
    laid by for a rainy day;
Safe in the hands of good men,
    and easy to get at;
Put in another clause there,
    and give her half of that.

Yes, I see you smile, Sir,
    at my givin' her so much;
Yes, divorce is cheap, Sir,
    but I take no stock in such!
True and fair I married her,
    when she was blithe and young;
And Betsy was al'ays good to me,
    exceptin' with her tongue.

Once, when I was young as you,
    and not so smart, perhaps,
For me she smittened a lawyer,
    and several other chaps;
And all of them was flustered,
    and fairly taken down,
And I for a time was counted
    the luckiest man in town.

Once when I had a fever—
    I won't forget it soon—
I was hot as a basted turkey
    and crazy as a loon;
Never an hour went by me
    when she was out of sight—
She nursed me true and tender,
    and stuck to me day and night.

And if ever a house was tidy,
    and ever a kitchen clean,
Her house and kitchen was tidy
    as any I ever seen;
And I don't complain of Betsy,
    or any of her acts,
Exceptin' when we've quarreled,
    and told each other facts.

And so draw up the papers, lawyer,
    and I'll go home to-night,
And read the agreement to her,
    and see if it's all right;
And then, in the mornin',
    I'll sell to a tradin' man I know,
And kiss the child that was left to us,
    and out in the world I'll go.

And one thing put in the paper,
    that first to me didn't occur;
That when I am dead at last
    she'll bring me back to her;
And lay me under the maples
    I planted years ago,
When she and I were happy
    before we quarreled so.

And when she dies I wish that she
    would be laid by me,
And lyin' together in silence,
    perhaps we will agree;
And if ever we meet in heaven,
    I wouldn't think it queer
If we loved each other better
    because we quarreled here.

How Betsy and I Made Up

By Will Carleton

Give us your hand, Mr. Lawyer;
   how do you do today?
You drew up that paper—
   I suppose you want your pay.
Don't cut down your figures;
   make it an X or a V;
For that 'ere written agreement
   was just the makin' of me.

Goin' home that evenin'
   I tell you I was blue,
Thinkin' of all my troubles,
   and what I was goin' to do;
And if my hosses hadn't been
   the steadiest team alive,
They'd 've tipped me over certain,
   for I couldn't see where to drive.

No—for I was a laborin'
   under a heavy load;
No—for I was travelin'
   an entirely different road;
For I was a-tracin' over
   the path of our lives ag'in,
And seein' where we missed the way,
   and where we might have been.

And many a corner we'd turned
   that just to a quarrel led,
When I ought to 've held my temper,
   and driven straight ahead;
And the more I thought it over
   the more these memories came,
And the more I struck the opinion
   that I was most to blame.

And things I had long forgotten
   kept risin' in my mind,
Of little matters betwixt us,
   where Betsy was good and kind;
And these things flashed all through me,
   as you know things sometimes will
When a feller's alone in the darkness,
   and every thing is still.

"But," says I, "we're too far along
   to take another track.
And when I put my hand to the plow
   I do not oft turn back;

And tain't an uncommon thing now
   for couples to smash in two";
And so I set my teeth together,
   and vowed I'd see it through.

When I come in sight o' the house
   'twas some at in the night,
And just as I turned a hill-top
   I see the kitchen light
Which often a han'some pictur'
   to a hungry person makes,
But it don't interest a feller much
   that's goin' to pull up stakes.

And when I went in the house
   the table was set for me—
As good a supper's I ever saw;
   or ever want to see;
And I crammed the agreement down
   my pocket as well as I could,
And fell to eatin' my victuals,
   which somehow didn't taste good.

And Betsy, she pretended
   to look about the house,
But she watched my side coat pocket
   like a cat would watch a mouse;
And then she went to foolin'
   a little with her cup,
And intently readin' a paper,
   a-holdin' it wrong side up.

And when I'd done my supper
   I drawed the agreement out,
And give it to her without a word,
   for she knowed what 'twas about;
And then I hummed a little tune,
   but now and then a note,
Was busted by some animal
   that hopped up in my throat.

Then Betsy she got her specs
   from off the mantel-shelf,
And read the article over
   quite softly to herself;
Read it by little and little,
   for her eyes is getting old,
And lawyers' writin' ain't no print,
   especially when it's cold.

And after she'd read a little
  she gave my arm a touch,
And kindly said she was afraid
  I was 'lowin' her too much;
But when she was through she went for me,
  her face a-streamin' with tears,
And kissed me for the first time
  in over twenty years!

I don't know what you'll think, Sir—
  I didn't come to inquire—
But I picked up that agreement
  and stuffed it in the fire;
And told her we'd bury that hatchet
  alongside of the cow;
And we struck to an agreement
  never to have another row.

And I told her in the future
  I wouldn't speak cross or rash
If half the crockery in the house
  was broken all to smash;
And she said, in regards to heaven,
  we'd try and learn its worth
By startin' a branch establishment
  and runnin' it here on earth.

And so we sat a-talkin'
  three quarters of the night,
And opened our hearts to each other
  until they both grew light;
And the days when I was winnin' her
  away from so many men
Was nothin' to that evenin'
  I courted her over again.

Next mornin' an ancient virgin
  took pains to call on us,
Her lamp all trimmed and a-burnin'
  to kindle another fuss;
But when she went to pryin'
  and openin' of old sores,
My Betsy rose politely,
  and showed her out of doors.

Since then I don't deny
  but there's a word or two;
But we've got our eyes wide open,
  and know just what to do;

When one speaks cross the other
  just meets it with a laugh,
And the first one's ready to give up
  considerable more than half.

Maybe you'll think me soft, Sir,
  a-talkin' in this style,
But somehow it does me lots of good
  to tell it once in a while;
And I do it for a compliment—
  'tis so that you can see
That that-there written agreement of yours
  was just the makin' of me.

So make out your bill, Mr. Lawyer;
  don't stop short of an X;
Make it more if you want to,
  for I have got the checks.
I'm richer than a National Bank,
  with all its treasures told,
For I've got a wife at home now
  that's worth her weight in gold.

> *Editor's Note: This sequel to "Betsy and I Are Out" is another of Carleton's attempts to make a happy ending out of one of his original works. In this one, the narrator returns to the lawyer to explain that his divorce decree is no longer needed.—K.T.*

Young Charlotte

By William Lorenzo Carter

Young Charlotte lived by the mountainside
In a lone and dreary spot.
No dwelling there, for five miles round,
Except her father's cot;
But yet on many a winter's eve
Young swains would gather there,
For her father kept a social board
And she was very fair.

Her father loved to see her dressed
Fine as a city belle,
For she was the only child he had,
And he loved his daughter well.
'Twas New Year's Eve. The sun went down.
Wild looked her anxious eyes
Along the frosty window panes
To see the sleighs pass by.

At a village inn, fifteen miles round,
There's a merry ball to-night.
The air is freezing cold above,
But the hearts are warm and light.
And while she looked with longing eyes,
Then a well-known voice she hears,
And dashing up to the cottage door
Young Charley's sleigh appears.

Her mother says, "My daughter dear,
This blanket around you fold,
For it is a dreadful night abroad,
You'll take your death of cold."
"Oh, no! Oh, no!" young Charlotte said,
And she laughed like a gypsy queen.
"For to ride in blankets muffled up
I never would be seen.

"My silken cloak is quite enough.
'Tis lined, you know, throughout,
And then I have the silken scarf
To tie my face about."
Her gloves and bonnet being on,
She jumped into the sleigh
And away they ride o'er the mountainside
And o'er the hills away.

There's merry music in the bells
As o'er the hills they go,
For the creaking rake the runners make
As they bite the frozen snow.
Then o'er the hills and faster o'er
And by the cold starlight,
When Charles, in these few frozen words,
At last the silence broke:

"Such a night as this I never knew.
My reins I scarce can hold."
Young Charlotte said with a trembling voice,
"I am exceeding cold."
He cracked his whip which urged his steed
Much faster than before,
And then the other five miles round
In silence were rode o'er.

"How fast," says Charles, "the freezing ice
Is gathering on my brow."
Young Charlotte said with a feeble voice,
"I'm growing warmer now."
Then o'er the hills and faster o'er
And by the cold starlight
Until they reached the village inn
And the ballroom was in sight.

They reached the inn and Charles sprang out
And giving his hand to her,
"Why sit you like a monument
That has no power to stir?"
He called her once, he called her twice,
But yet she never stirred.
He called her name again and again,
But she answered not a word.

He took her hand in his. O God!
'Twas cold and hard as stone.
He tore the mantle from her brow
And the cold stars on her shone.
Then quickly to the lighted hall
Her lifeless form he bore,
For Charlotte was a frozen corpse
And a word she spake never more.

He knelt himself down by her side
And bitter tears did flow,
For he said, "My young intended bride,
I never more shall know."
He flung his arms around her neck
And kissed her marble brow.
His thoughts went back to the place she said,
"I'm growing warmer now."

He bore her out into the sleigh
And with her he rode home,
And when they reached the cottage door
Oh, how her parents mourned!
They mourned for the loss of their daughter dear,
And Charles mourned o'er the gloom
When Charles' heart with grief did break
They slumber in one tomb.

Two Little Girls in Blue

Author Unknown

An old man gazed on a photograph,
In a locket he'd worn for years,
His nephew then asked him the reason why—
This picture had caused him tears.

"Just listen," he said, "and I'll tell you, lad,
A story that's strange, but true,
Your Father and I, at the school, one day—
Met two little girls in blue.

"Two little girls in blue, lad,
Two little girls in blue,
They were sisters, we were brothers,
And learned to love those two.
One little girl in blue, lad,
who won your Father's heart,
Became your Mother,
I married the other—
But we have drifted apart.

"That picture was one of those girls," he said,
"And the least she was once a wife,
I caught her unfaithful, we quarreled, lad—
And parted that night for life.

"My fancy or jealousy wronged a heart,
A heart that was good and true,
For two better girls never lived, than they—
Those two little girls in blue."

Butcher Boy

Author Unknown

In Jersey City, where I did dwell,
A butcher boy I loved so well—
He courted me, my life away
And then with me, he would not stay.
Oh Mother, Mother, you do not know
What grief and pain and sorrow, woe,
Go bring a chair and set me down,
A pen and ink to write it on.
And on my breast a turtle dove
To show this world, I died for love.

Curfew Must Not Ring Tonight

by Rose Hartwick Thorpe

Slowly England's sun was setting
　o'er the hilltops far away,
Filling all the land with beauty
　at the close of one sad day;
And the last rays kissed the forehead
　of a man and maiden fair,
He with footsteps slow and weary,
　she with sunny floating hair;
He with bowed head,
　sad and thoughtful,
　she with lips all cold and white,
Struggling to keep back the murmur,
　"Curfew must not ring tonight!"

"Sexton," Bessie's white lips faltered,
　pointing to the prison old,
With its turrets tall and gloomy, with
　its walls, dark, damp and cold—
"I've a lover in the prison,
　doomed this very night to die
At the ringing of the curfew,
　and no earthly help is nigh.
Cromwell will not come till sunset";
　and her face grew strangely white
As she breathed the husky whisper,
　"Curfew must not ring tonight!"

"Bessie," calmly spoke the sexton—
　and his accents pierced her heart
Like the piercing of an arrow,
　like a deadly poisoned dart—
"Long, long years I've rung the curfew
　from that gloomy, shadowed tower;
Every evening, just as sunset,
　it has told the twilight hour;

I have done my duty ever,
　tried to do it just and right—
Now I'm old I still must do it:
　Curfew, girl, must ring tonight!"

Wild her eyes and pale her features,
　stern and white her thoughtful brow,
And within her secret bosom
　Bessie made a solemn vow.
She had listened while the judges read,
　without a tear or sigh,
"At the ringing of the curfew,
　Basil Underwood must die."
And her breath came fast and faster,
　and her eyes grew large and bright,
As in undertone she murmured,
　"Curfew must not ring tonight!"

With quick step she bounded forward,
　sprang within the old church door,
Left the old man treading slowly paths
　he'd often trod before;
Not one moment paused the maiden,
　but with eye and cheek aglow
Mounted up the gloomy tower,
　where the bell swung to and fro
As she climbed the dusty ladder,
　on which fell no ray of light,
Up and up, her white lips saying,
　"Curfew must not ring tonight!"

She has reached the topmost ladder,
　o'er her hangs the great dark bell:
Awful is the gloom beneath her
　like the pathway down to hell;

Lo, the ponderous tongue is swinging.
    'Tis the hour of curfew now,
And the sight has chilled her bosom,
    stopped her breath and paled her brow;
Shall she let it ring? No, never!
    Flash her eyes with sudden light,
And she springs and grasps it firmly:
    "Curfew shall not ring tonight!"

Out she swung, far out; the city
    seemed a speck of light below;
She 'twixt heaven and earth suspended
    as the bell swung to and fro;
And the sexton at the bell rope,
    old and deaf, heard not the bell,
But he thought it still was ringing fair
    young Basil's funeral knell.
Still the maiden clung more firmly,
    and, with trembling lips and white,
Said to hush her heart's wild beating,
    "Curfew shall not ring tonight!"

It was o'er; the bell ceased swaying,
    and the maiden stepped once more
Firmly on the ladder,
    where for hundred years before
Human foot had not been planted;
    but the brave deed she had done
Should be told long ages after—
    often as the setting sun
Should illume the sky with beauty,
    aged sires, with heads of white,
Long should tell the little children,
    "Curfew did not ring that night."

O'er the distant hills came Cromwell;
    Bessie sees him, and her brow,
Full of hope and full of gladness,
    has no anxious traces now.

At his feet she tells her story,
    shows her hands all bruised and torn;
And her face so sweet and pleading,
    yet with sorrow pale and worn,
Touched his heart with sudden pity—
    lit his eye with misty light;
"Go, your lover lives!" said Cromwell;
    "Curfew shall not ring tonight!"

Towser Shall Be Tied Tonight

Author Unknown

Editor's Note: *This humorous parody of Thorpe's "Curfew Must Not Ring Tonight" was written by some unknown poet not long after the original version appeared. Both versions are oft requested in the pages of* Good Old Days *magazine.—K.T.*

Slow the Kansas sun was setting,
O'er the wheat fields far away,
Streaking all the air with cobwebs
At the close of one hot day;
And the last rays kissed the forehead
Of a man and maiden fair,
He with whiskers short and frowsy,
She with red and glistening hair,
He with shut jaws stern and silent;
She, with lips all cold and white,
Struggled to keep back the murmur,
"Towser shall be tied tonight."

"Papa," slowly spoke the daughter,
"I am almost seventeen,
And I have a real true lover,
Though he's rather young and green;
But he has a horse and buggy,
And a cow, and thirty hens,—
Boys that start out poor, dear Papa,
Make the best of honest men.
But if Towser sees and bites him,
Fills his heart with sudden fright,
He will never come again, Pa;
Towser must be tied tonight."

"Daughter," firmly spoke the farmer,
(Every word pierced her young heart,
Like a carving knife through chicken
As it hunts the tender parts)—
"I've a patch of early melons,
Two of them are ripe today;

Towser must be loose to watch them
Or they'll all be stole away.
I have hoed them late and early
In dim morn and evening light;
Now they're grown I must not lose them;
Towser'll not be tied tonight."

Then the old man ambled forward,
Opened wide the kennel-door,
Towser bounded forth to meet him
As he oft had done before.
And the farmer stooped and loosed him
From the dog-chain short and stout;
To himself he softly chuckled,
"Bessie's feller must look out."
But the maiden at the window
Saw the cruel teeth snow-white;
In an undertone she murmured,—
"Towser must be tied tonight."

Then the maiden's brow grew thoughtful
And her breath came short and quick,
Till she spied the family clothesline,
And she whispered, "That's the trick."
From the kitchen door she glided
With a plate of meat and bread;
Towser wagged his tail in greeting,
Knowing well he would be fed,
In his well-worn leather collar,
Tied she then the clothesline tight,
All the time her white lips saying:
"Towser shall be tied tonight."

"There, old doggie," spoke the maiden,
"You can watch the melon patch,
But the front gate's free and open,
When John Henry lifts the latch.
For the clothesline tight is fastened

To the harvest apple tree,
You can run and watch the melons,
But the front gate you can't see."
Then her glad ears hear a buggy,
And her eyes grow big and bright,
While her young heart says in gladness,
"Towser dog is tied tonight."

Up the path the young man saunters
With his eyes and cheeks aglow;
For he loves the red-haired maiden
And he aims to tell her so.
Bessie's roguish little brother,
In a fit of boyish glee,
Had untied the slender clothesline,
From the harvest apple tree.
Then old Towser heard the footsteps,
Raised his bristles, fixed for a fight,—
"Bark away," the maiden whispers;
"Towser, you are tied tonight."

Then old Towser bounded forward,
Passed the open kitchen door;
Bessie screamed and quickly followed,
But John Henry's gone before.
Down the path he speeds most quickly,
For old Towser sets the pace;
And the maiden close behind them
Shows them she is in the race.
Then the clothesline, can she get it?
And her eyes grow big and bright;
And she springs and grasps it firmly:
"Towser shall be tied tonight."

Often times a little minute
Forms the destiny of men.
You can change the fate of nations
By the stroke of one small pen.
Towser made one last long effort,
Caught John Henry by the pants,
But John Henry kept on running
For he thought that his last chance.

But the maiden held on firmly,
And the rope was drawn up tight.
But old Towser kept the garments,
For he was not tied that night.

Then the father hears the racket;
With long strides he soon is there,
When John Henry and the maiden,
Crouching, for the worst prepare.
At his feet John tells his story,
Shows his clothing soiled and torn;
And his face so sad and pleading,
Yet so white and scared and worn,
Touched the old man's heart with pity,
Filled his eyes with misty light.
"Take her, boy, and make her happy,—
Towser shall be tied tonight."

The Face on the Bar-Room Floor

By Hugh Antoine D'Arcy

'Twas a balmy summer evening,
 and a goodly crowd was there,
Which well-nigh filled Joe's bar-room,
 on the corner of the square;
And as songs and witty stories
 came through the open door,
A vagabond crept slowly in
 and posed upon the floor.

"Where did it come from?" someone said.
 "The wind has blown it in."
"What does it want?" another cried.
 "Some whisky, rum or gin?"
"Here, Toby, seek him, if your stomach's
 equal to the work—
I wouldn't touch him with a fork,
 he's filthy as a Turk."

This badinage the poor wretch
 took with stoical good grace;
In fact, he smiled as tho'
 he thought he'd struck the
 proper place.

"Come, boys, I know there's kindly hearts
 among so good a crowd—
To be in such good company
 would make a deacon proud.

"Give me a drink—that's what I want—
 I'm out of funds, you know,
When I had cash to treat the gang
 this hand was never slow.
What? You laugh as if you thought
 this pocket never held a sou;
I once was fixed as well, my boys,
 as any one of you.

"There, thanks, that's braced me nicely;
 God bless you one and all;
Next time I pass this good saloon
 I'll make another call.
Give you a song? No, I can't do that;
 my singing days are past;
My voice is cracked, my throat's worn out,
 and my lungs are going fast.

"Say! Give me another whiskey,
 and I'll tell you what I'll do—
I'll tell you a funny story,
 and a fact, I promise, too,
That ever I was a decent man
 not one of you would think;
But I was, some four or five years back.
 Say, give me another drink.

"Fill her up, Joe, I want to put
 some life into my frame—
Such little drinks to a bum
 like me are miserably tame;
Five fingers—there, that's the scheme—
 and corking whiskey, too.
Well, here's luck, boys, and landlord,
 my best regards to you.

"You've treated me pretty kindly
  and I'd like to tell you how
I came to be the dirty sot
  you see before you now.
As I told you, once I was a man,
  with a muscle, frame and health,
And, but for a blunder ought to have
  made considerable wealth.

"I was a painter—not one that daubed
  on bricks and wood,
But an artist, and for my age,
  was rated pretty good.
I worked hard at my canvas,
  and was bidding fair to rise,
For gradually I saw the star
  of fame before my eyes.

"I made a picture perhaps you've seen,
  'tis called the 'Chase of Fame.'
It brought me fifteen hundred pounds
  and added to my name.
And then I met a woman—
  now comes the funny part—
With eyes that petrified my brain,
  and sunk into my heart.

"Why don't you laugh? 'Tis funny that
  the vagabond you see
Could ever love a woman,
  and expect her love for me;
But 'twas so, and for a month or two
  her smiles were freely given,
And when her loving lips touched mine,
  it carried me to heaven.

"Boys, did you ever see a girl
  for whom your soul you'd give,
With a form like the Milo Venus,
  too beautiful to live;
With eyes that would beat the Koh-i-noor,
  and a wealth of chestnut hair?
If so, 'twas she, for there never was
  another half so fair.

"I was working on a portrait,
  one afternoon in May,
Of a fair-haired boy, a friend of mine,
  who lived across the way;
And Madeline admired it, and,
  much to my surprise,
She said she'd like to know the man
  that had such dreamy eyes.

"It didn't take long to know him,
  and before the month had flown
My friend had stole my darling,
  and I was left alone;
And ere a year of misery
  had passed above my head,
The jewel I had treasured so
  had tarnished, and was dead.

"That's why I took to drink, boys.
  Why, I never saw you smile,
I thought you'd be amused,
  and laughing all the while.
Why, what's the matter, friend?
  There's a tear-drop in your eye,
Come, laugh, like me; 'tis only babes
  and women that should cry.

"Say, boys, if you give me just another
  whiskey I'll be glad,
And I'll draw right here a picture
  of the face that drove me mad.
Give me that piece of chalk with which
  you mark the baseball score—
You shall see the lovely Madeline
  upon the bar-room floor."

Another drink, and with chalk in hand,
  the vagabond began
To sketch a face that might well buy
  the soul of any man.
Then, as he placed another lock
  upon the shapely head,
With a fearful shriek he leaped and fell
  across the picture—dead.

Home & the Old Folks

Chapter Six

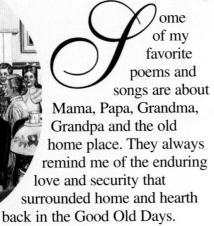

Some of my favorite poems and songs are about Mama, Papa, Grandma, Grandpa and the old home place. They always remind me of the enduring love and security that surrounded home and hearth back in the Good Old Days. Whether farm or small town, rural or urban, home and the old folks provided a cocoon of warmth, love and protection for the little ones as we grew.

In today's modern life of so many disjointed families, many children are raised in a home with just one parent. The only time I heard of that as a youngster was when there was some sort of tragedy. I remember when the father of one of my best friends, Chet, died when we were about 16. I had no idea how life could go on without a father, and it was the first time I was exposed to the harsh realities of that possibility.

My own life, frankly, was idyllic. Mama, Daddy and we three kids lived peaceably—most of the time at least—under the only roof I ever knew growing up. That old home grew up as we did. Daddy built two small rooms—a kitchen and a bedroom—when he and Mama married.

My brother came along first; soon after I was born Daddy added a living room. Two years later there was a little sister, but those three rooms continued to supply our needs until I was almost 12. Then, with the help of two brothers, Daddy added two more bedrooms and—to all our amazement and joy—indoor plumbing and a bathroom!

That was the home that housed the love that Mama and Daddy built together until his death, just a month short of their golden wedding anniversary.

It wasn't just our immediate family that made life so secure in those days.

Grandma Stamps, who had been widowed when Mama was but a baby, lived in a tiny frame house with my Uncle Bob less than a quarter mile away.

Grandma and Grandpa Tate lived much farther away—or at least it seemed that way in my youth. In reality it was about three miles or so—just a jalopy ride with a few puddles to jump.

Just as Grandma Stamps relied on Uncle Bob and Mama, Grandma and Grandpa Tate relied on their brood as well. (Remember, there was no Social Security or social welfare in those days.) Three of their children lived a matter of a few hundred yards from them. Of the dozen children Grandma and Grandpa Tate raised to adulthood, only two moved out of the county.

When Janice and I married, we lived within a few minutes of Mama and Daddy, and within walking distance of Janice's parents. She was an only child and both of us had been raised to take care of our own, so it was only natural that we would come to help care for those who had cared for us so well as we grew.

Just like the song "M-O-T-H-E-R" below, all the verse in this chapter is dedicated to those helped bring us up in comfort and love. I know you will enjoy these poems and songs of Home and the Old Folks.

—*Ken Tate*

M-O-T-H-E-R

Howard Johnson

M is for the many things she gave me,
O means only that she's growing old.
T is for the tears she shed to save me,
H is for her heart of purest gold.
E is for her eyes with lovelight shining,
R means right and right she'll always be.
Put them all together, they spell Mother,
A word that means the world to me.

Me an' Pap an' Mother

By Strickland W. Gillian

When I was a little tike
I set at th' table 'tween
   my mother an' my Pap:
Eat all I was able.
Pap he fed me on one side,
Mammy on th' other,
Tell ye we was chums, them days—
Me an' Pap an' Mother.

Sundays, we'd take great, long walks
Through th' woods an' pasters;
Pap he al'ays packed a cane,
Mother 'n' me picked asters.
Sometimes they 's a sister 'long,
Sometimes they 's a brother;
But they al'ays was us three—
Me an' Pap an' Mother.

Pap he didn't gabble much;
Hel' his head down, thinkin'.
Didn't seem t' hear us talk,
Nor the cow-bells clinkin'.
Love-streaks all 'peared worried out
'Bout one thing er 'nuther;
Didn't al'ays
   understand Pap—
That's me an' Mother.

I got big an' went away;
Left th' farm behind me.
Thinkin' o' that partin' yit
Seems t' choke
   an' blind me.
Course I'd be all
   safe an' good
With m' married brother,
But we had to part,
   us three—
Me an' Pap an' Mother.

Hurried back, one day;
   found Pap—
Changed, an' pale
   an' holler;
Seen right off he'd have
   to go—

Where we couldn't foller.
Lovin' streaks all showed up then—
Ah, we loved each other,
Talked fast, just t' keep back tears—
Me an' Pap an' Mother.

Pap he's dead; but Mother ain't;
Soon will be, I reckon;
Claims already she can see
Pap's forefinger beckon.
Life hain't long, I'll go myself
One these days eruther,
Then we'll have good times again,
Me an' Pap an' Mother.

Purtier hills we'll have t' climb,
Saunterin' long old fashion,
Hear th' wild birds singing 'round;
See th' river splashin—
If God'd only let us three
Be' lone, like we'd ruther,
Heaven'd be a great ol' place
For me an' Pap an' Mother.

When Mama Was a Little Girl

Author Unknown

When Mama was a little girl,
  before I came to town,
She was so good, you'd tho't she would be
  wearing soon a crown;
She'd never kiss the boys, you bet;
  good gracious, no,
She'd only let the boys kiss her,
  she was a pearl,
When Mama was a little girl.

Chorus:
When Mama was a little girl,
'Twould take a prince, a duke, or earl,
To make her raise her modest eyes,
Oh, Mama was a prize.

When Mama was a little girl,
  no bustle did she wear;
Nor high heeled boots or tailored suits,
  nor did she bang her hair;
She was quiet as a mouse,
  she never romped around the house;
At eight o'clock in bed she'd curl,
  when Mama was a little girl.

When Mama was a little girl,
  she never went to balls;
I here assert she did not flirt,
  or waste her time in calls;
She never used a word of slang,
  old-fashioned hymns all day she sang;
She never in the waltz did whirl,
  when Mama was a little girl.

When Mama was a little girl
  she never stayed out late;
She did not talk with boys or walk,
  or swing upon the gate;
My stars; she was too good for that;
She disapproved of idle chat;
Indeed she was a rare, rare pearl,
  when Mama was a little girl.

When Pa Was Young

Author Unknown

Boys were so queer
  when Pa was young,
They always liked to work;
They never seemed to want to play
And never tried to shirk;
They were so mannerly and nice,
And just as good as pie,
The wonder is they ever lived
Since good boys mostly die.

They never made a racket in
The house or on the street,
And never came inside the door
With dirt upon their feet;
They never stumbled over chairs
Or wrestled in the house,
They were as noiseless as a cat
That's hunting for a mouse.

They never fought with pillows when
They went to bed at night,
They just crept softly up the stairs
And seldom took a light;
They never had to be waked up,
But when the rooster crew
They sprang right out,
  put on their clothes
And down the steps they flew.

When school time came,
  away they went,
As happy as a king,
And studied, my how they did dig
And mastered everything.

Sometimes at noon they would forget
Their dinner and their skates,
And stay right at their desks to work
With pencils and with slates.

They never even looked at girls,
Oh no, they didn't care,
For sparkling eyes and rosy cheeks
And fluffy golden hair.
They kept their eyes right on the book
And mastered every rule,
They didn't even seem to know
There was a girl in school.

They never had to be kept in
For anything they'd done,
They knew what they
  were sent there for,
They didn't go for fun.
I wish I'd lived when Pa was young,
Things were so different then,
For all the boys were studious then
And acted just like men.

My Uncle Dan, he comes sometimes
To visit us awhile,
And when I tell him how it was
You ought to see him smile;
He never says a word, you know
But acts just like he thought
There were some things
  that boys did then
      WHICH MY PA
          HAS FORGOT!

My Mother Was a Lady

Author Unknown

Two drummers they were seated
In a grand hotel one day,
Just smiling and a-cracking jokes
In a friendly sort of way.
There came a pretty waitress
To bring a tray of food.
They spoke to her familiarly,
In a manner rather rude.
At first she did not notice
Nor make the least reply,
But one remark was made
   to her
Brought teardrops to her
   eyes.
She turned on her
   tormentors.
Her cheeks were blushing
   red,
Approaching as a picture,
And this is what she said:
  "My mother was a lady,
And yours you would allow,
And you may have a sister,
Who needs protection now.
I've come to this great city

To seek my brother dear,
And you wouldn't dare insult me, Sir,
   If Brother Jack were here."

    The two sat there in silence,
    Their heads hung down in
     shame,
  "Forgive us, Miss, we meant no harm.
  Pray tell me what's your name."
She told him and he cried aloud,
"I know your brother, too!
We've been friends for many years,
And he often speaks of you.
 Come go with me when I go back,
  And if you'll only wed,
   I'll take you to him as my bride,
   For I've loved since you said,
   'My mother was a lady,
  And yours you would allow,
And you may have a sister
Who needs protection now.
I've come to this great city
To seek my brother dear,
And you wouldn't dare insult me, Sir,
If Brother Jack were here.' "

Nobody Knows But Mother

By H.C. Dodge

Nobody knows of the work it makes
To keep the home together;
Nobody knows of the steps it takes,
Nobody knows—but Mother.

Nobody listens to childish woes
Which kisses only smother;
Nobody's pained by naughty blows,
Nobody—but Mother.

Nobody knows of the sleepless care
Bestowed on baby brother;
Nobody knows of the tender pray'r,
Nobody—only Mother.

Nobody knows of the lessons taught
Of loving one another;
Nobody knows of the patience sought,
Nobody—only Mother.

Nobody knows of the anxious fears
Lest darling may not weather
The storm of life in after years,
Nobody knows—but Mother.

Nobody kneels at the throne above
To thank the heavenly Father,
For that sweetest gift—a mother's love;
Nobody can—but Mother.

Father, Dear Father

By Henry Clay Work

Father, dear Father, come home with me now!
The clock in the steeple strikes one.
You said you were coming
    right home from the shop,
As soon as your day's work was done.
Our fire has gone out, our house is all dark,
And Mother's been watching since tea,
With poor brother Benny so sick in her arms,
And no one to help her but me.
Come home, come home, come home!
Please Father, dear Father, come home!

Hear the sweet voice of the child, which,
The night winds repeat as they roam!
Oh, who could resist this most plaintive
    of prayers?
Please Father, dear Father, come home!

Father, dear Father, come home with me now!
The clock in the steeple strikes two;
The night has grown colder, and Benny is worse—

But he has been calling for you.
Indeed he is worse, Ma says he will die—
Perhaps before morning shall dawn;
And this is the message she sent me to bring—
"Come quickly or he will be gone."
Come home, come home, come home!
Please Father, dear Father, come home!

Father, dear Father, come home with me now!
The clock in the steeple strikes three;
The house is so lonely!—the hours are so long
For poor weeping Mother and me.
Yes, we are alone—poor Benny is dead;
And gone with the angels of light;
And these are the very last words that he said—
"I want to kiss Papa good night."
Come home, come home, come home!
Please Father, dear Father, come home!

For All Parents

By Edgar Guest

I'll lend you for a little time
    A child of mine, he said.
For you to love there as he lives,
    And mourn when he is dead.

It may be six or seven years,
    Or twenty-two or three.
But will you, 'til I call him back,
    Take care of him for me?

He'll bring his charms to gladden you,
    And shall his stay be brief.
You'll have his lovely memories,
    As solace for your grief.

I cannot promise he will stay,
    Since all from earth return.
But there are lessons taught down there,
    I want this child to learn.

I've searched the wide world over,
    In my search for teachers true.

And from the throngs that crowd life's lanes,
    I have selected you.

Now will you give him all your love,
    Nor think the labor vain.
Nor hate me when I come to call,
    To take him back again?

I fancied that I heard them say,
    Dear Lord, thy will be done.
For all the joy thy child shall bring,
    The risk of grief we'll run.

We'll shelter him with tenderness,
    We'll love him while we may.
And for the happiness we've known,
    Will ever grateful stay.

But shall the angels call for him,
    Much sooner than we planned.
We'll brave the bitter grief that comes,
    … And try to understand.

Papa's Letter

By Flora Page

I was sitting in my study,
Writing letters, when I heard,
"Please, dear Mama, Mary told me,
'Mama mustn't be disturbed.'

"But Ise tired of the kitty,
Want some offer thing to do.
Writing letters is fun, Mama.
Taint I write a letter, too?"

"Not now, Darling, Mama's busy,
Run and play with Kitty now."
"No, no, Mama, me write letter.
Tan if you will show me how."

I would paint my darling's picture
As his bright eyes searched my face:
Hair of gold and eyes of azure,
Form of childish witching grace.

But the eager face was clouded
As I slowly shook my head
Till I said, "I'll make a letter
Of you, darling boy, instead."

So I parted back the tresses
From his forehead big and white
And a stamp in sport I patted
Mid its waves of golden light.

Then I said, "Now little letter,
Go away and bear good news,"
And I smiled as down the staircase
Clattered loud the little shoes.

Leaving me, the darling hurried
Down to Mary in his glee.
"Mama's writing lots of letters.
Ise a letter, Mary, see!"

No one heard the little prattler
As once more he climbed the stair,
Reached his little cap and tippet,
Standing on the entry chair.

No one heard the front door open,
No one saw the golden hair

As it flowed o'er his shoulder
In the crisp October air.

Down the street the baby hastened,
Till he reached the office door.
"Ise a letter, Mr. Postman.
Is there any room for more?

"'Cause 'is letter's going to Papa.
Papa lives with God, you know.
Mama sent me for a letter,
Drive me one; thanks, I can go."

But the clerk in wonder answered,
"Not today, my little man."
"Den I find another office,
I must do it if I can."

Fain the clerk would have detained him.
But the pleading face was gone,
And little feet were hastening
By the busy crowd swept on.

Suddenly the crowd was parted,
People fled to left and right
As a pair of maddened horses
At a moment dashed in sight.

No one saw the baby figure,
No one saw the golden hair
Till a voice of frightened sweetness
Rang out on the autumn air.

Twas too late—a moment only
Stood the beauteous vision there,
Then the little face lay lifeless,
Covered o'er with golden hair.

Reverently they raised my darling,
Brushed away the curls of gold.
Saw the stamp upon his forehead,
Growing now so icy cold.

Not a mark the face disfigured,
Showing where a hoof had trod.
But the little life was ended.
Papa's letter was with God.

Somebody's Mother

By Mary Dow Brine

The woman was old and ragged and gray
And bent with the chill of the Winter's day.
The street was wet with a recent snow
And the woman's feet were aged and slow.
She stood at the crossing and waited long,
Alone, uncared for, amid the throng
Of human beings who passed her by
Nor heeded the glance of her anxious eye.
Down the street, with laughter and shout,
Glad in the freedom of "school let out,"
Came the boys like a flock of sheep,
Hailing the snow piled white and deep.
Past the woman so old and gray
Hastened the children on their way.
Nor offered a helping hand to her—
So meek, so timid, afraid to stir,
Lest the carriage wheels or the horses' feet
Should crowd her down in the slippery street.

At last came one of the merry troop,
The gayest laddie of all the group;
He paused beside her, and whispered low:
"I'll help you across if you wish to go."
Her aged hand on his strong young arm
She placed, and so, without hurt or harm,
He guided the trembling feet along,
Proud that his own were firm and strong,
Then back again to his friends he went,
His young heart happy and well content.
"She's somebody's mother, boys, you know,
For all she's aged and poor and slow.
And I hope some fellow will lend a hand
To help my mother, you understand,
If ever she's poor and old and gray,
When her own dear boy is far away."
And "somebody's mother" bowed low her head
In her home that night, and the prayer she said
Was "God be kind to the noble boy,
Who is somebody's son, and pride and joy!"
Faint was her voice, worn and weak,
But the Father hears, when His children speak.
And Angels caught the faltering words,
And somebody's mother's prayer was heard.

Silver-Haired Daddy of Mine

Author Unknown

*In a vine-covered shack in the
mountain,*
Bravely fighting the battle of time
*Is a dear one who's weathered
life's sorrows,*
'Tis that silver-haired Daddy of mine.
If I could recall all the heartaches,
Dear old Daddy, I've caused you to bear,
If I could erase those lines on your face
And bring back the gold to your hair,
If God would but grant me the power,
Just to turn back the pages of time,
I'd give all I own if I could but atone,
To that silver-haired Daddy of mine.
I know it's too late, dear old Daddy,
To repay for the sorrow and care
But dear Mother is waiting in Heaven
Just to comfort and solace you there.

Hello Central, Give Me Heaven

Author Unknown

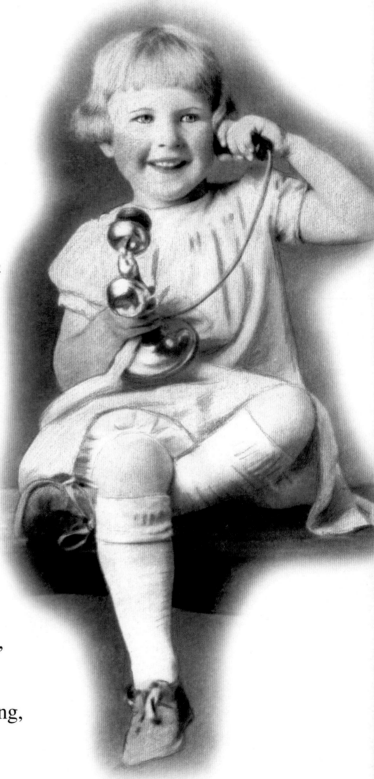

"Papa, I'm so sad and lonely,"
Sobbed a tearful little child,
"Since dear Mama's gone to
   Heaven
Papa, darling, you'll not smile.
I will speak to her and tell her
That we want her to come home,
You must listen and I'll call her,
On the telephone."

Chorus:
"Hello, Central, give me Heaven
For my Mama's there;
You will find her with the angels
On the golden stair;
Won't you tell her, it's me who's
   speaking?
Call her, won't you please;
For I want to surely tell her,
We're so lonely here?"

When the girl received the
   message
Coming through the telephone,
How her heart beat at the
   moment,
And the wires seemed to moan;
I will tell you that I've found her,
"Yes, dear heart, I'm coming
   home."
"Kiss me, Mama, kiss your darling,
Through the telephone."

Somebody's Darling

By Marie Ravenal DeLacoste

Into a ward of the white-washed hall
Where the dead and dying lay
Wounded by bayonets, shells and balls,
Somebody's darling was borne one day;
Somebody's darling so young and brave,
Wearing yet on his pale sweet face,
Soon to be hid by the dust of the grave,
The lingering light of his boyhood's grace.

Matted and damp are the curls of gold,
Kissing the snow of that fair young brow;
Pale are the lips of delicate mold—
Somebody's darling is dying now.
Back from his beautiful blue-veined brow,
Brush all the wondering waver of gold;
Cross his hands on his bosom now;
Somebody's darling is still and cold.

Kiss him once for somebody's sake,
Murmur a prayer soft and low;
One bright curl from its fair mates take;
They were somebody's pride, you know.

Somebody's hand has rested there,
Was it a mother soft and white?
And have the life of a sister fair
Been baptized in the waver of light?

God knows best he was somebody's love,
Somebody's heart enshrined him there,
Somebody wafted his name above,
Night and morn on the wings of prayer.
Somebody wept when he marched away,
Looking so handsome, brave and grand;
Somebody's kiss on his forehead lay,
Somebody clung to his parting hand.

Somebody's waiting and watching for him
Yearning to hold him again to her heart
And there he lies with his blue eyes dim,
And the smiling child like life apart.
Tenderly bury the fair young dead
Pausing to drop on his grave a tear;
Carve on the wooden slab at his head.
"Somebody's darling slumbers here."

Just Plain Folks *Author Unknown*

To a mansion in a city came a couple old and gray
To greet their son who'd left them long ago.
He had prospered and grown wealthy,
Since in youth he'd ran away.
And now his life was one of pomp and show.
Rich friends were by his side
Who had often heard him boast of folks so grand.
But the old man looked at him
    and said in modest pride
As he gently took his dear wife by the hand:

Chorus
"We are just plain folks, your mother here and me.
Just plain folks like our own folks used to be.
As our presence seems to grieve you,
    we will go away and leave you.
For we're sadly out of place here,
    for we're just plain folks.

"Not so long ago when you
    were but a simple
    country lad,
And did the work a
    country lad should do,
In those days you never
    looked with shame on
    Mother and old Dad.
In fact, my boy, we both
    were proud of you.
But something must have
    changed you, for your
    wealth has brought vain pride.
Still riches sometimes take swift wings they say;
But you'll always find a hearty welcome
    at your parents' side.
They will greet you in the same old loving way."

Don't Make Me Go to Bed and I'll Be Good

By Hugh Cross

A laughing baby boy, one ev'ning in his play,
Disturbed the household with his noisy glee;
I warned him to be good,
But he soon did disobey,
For he would soon forget a word from me.
I called him to my side and said,
"Son, you must go to bed;
'Cause your conduct has been very,
  very rude."
With trembling lips and tear-filled eyes,
  he pleaded with me;
"Don't make me go to bed and I'll be good."

"Don't, Papa, and I'll be good;
Don't, Papa, and I'll be good."
That's what I heard him say,
And it haunts me night and day.
"Don't make me go to bed and I'll be good."
Our lives had just been gladdened
  by his bright ascending beams,
Our boy now in our hearts was very dear;
I hastened to his bed and found him
  talking in his sleep;
He didn't seem to know that we were near.

I took him in my arms and found
  his body racked with pain;
To ease his pain we did the best we could;
It broke my heart to hear him
  crying loudly in his sleep:
"Don't make me go to bed and I'll be good."

How sorrow fills our heart,
  how fears oppress our mind,
When danger gathers 'round the ones we love,
He lingered but a day, then his spirit passed
  away,
To join the angel chorus up above.
All night and day we watched and prayed,
  We never left his side;
    To give him up, it seemed
      we never could;
      It broke my heart to hear him saying
        just before he died:
      "Don't make me go to bed
        and I'll be good."

Which Shall It Be?

By Ethel Lynn Beers

"Which shall it be? Which shall it be?"
I look'd at John—John look'd at me
(Dear, patient John, who loves me yet
As well as though my locks were jet);
And when I found that I must speak,
My voice seem'd strangely low and weak:
"Tell me again what Robert said."
And then I, listening, bent my head.

"This is his letter: 'I will give
A house and land while you shall live,
If, in return, from out your seven,
One child to me for aye is given.' "

I look'd at John's old garments worn
I thought of all that John had borne
Of poverty and work and care,
Which I, though willing, could not share;
I thought of seven mouths to feed;
Of seven little children's need,

And then of this. "Come, John," said I,
"We'll choose among them as they lie
Asleep"; so walking hand in hand,
Dear John and I survey'd our band.

First to the cradle lightly stepp'd,
Where the new nameless baby slept.
"Shall it be Baby?" whispered John.
I took his hand, and hurried on
To Lily's crib. Her sleeping grasp
Held her old doll within its clasp;
Her dark curls lay like gold alight,
A glory 'gainst the pillow white.
Softly her father stoop'd to lay
His rough hand down in loving way
When dream or whisper made her stir,
Then huskily said John, "Not her—not her!"

We stopp'd beside the trundle-bed,
And one long ray of lamplight shed
Athwart the boyish faces there,

In sleep so pitiful and fair;
I saw on Jamie's rough red cheek
A tear undried. Ere John could speak,
"He's but a baby, too," said I,
And kiss'd him as we hurried by.

Pale, patient Robbie's angel face
Still in his sleep bore suffering's trace.
"No, for a thousand crowns, not him!"
We whisper'd, while our eyes were dim.

Poor Dick! bad Dick! our wayward son,
Turbulent, reckless, idle one—
Could he be spared? Nay; He who gave
Bids us befriend him to his grave;
Only a mother's heart can be
Patient enough for such as he;
"And so," said John, "I would not dare
To send him from her bedside prayer."

Then stole we softly up above
And knelt by Mary, child of love.
"Perhaps for her 'twould better be,"
I said to John. Quite silently
He lifted up a curl astray
Across her cheek in willful way,
And shook his head: "Nay, love; not thee,"
The while my heart beat audibly.

Only one more, our eldest lad,
Trustly and truthful, good and glad—
So like his father. "No, John, no—
I cannot, will not, let him go."

And so we wrote, in courteous way,
We could not give one child away;
And afterward toil lighter seem'd
Thinking of that of which we dream'd,
Happy in truth that not one face
We miss'd from its accustom'd place;
Thankful to work for all the seven,
Trusting the rest to One in heaven.

The Boy Is Comin' Home

By John Mervin Hall

I tell you it is busy times
  jest now for me and Marm,
The boy is comin' home to spend
  Thanksgivin' on the farm;
'Tis ten long years since he went West
  to mingle in its strife,
He's done first-rate, and furthermore,
  he's got a western wife.
We got the letter yesterday,
  and Marm, she laid awake
Full half the night to praise the Lord
  and think what she must bake,
If I should feed the turkey now
  as she declares I must,
Why, long before Thanksgivin'
  he would swell all up and bust;
I've had to grind the choppin' knife
  and go ter choppin' mince,
And things are brewin'
  rich and fine
  and fit to feed a
  prince.
The boy, he writ for
  chicken pie,
  "with double
  crust," says he,

"And mixed with cream, that lovely pie
  you used to make for me."
He wants a big red apple
  from the hillside Northern Spy,
And butternuts—I've got 'em round
  the stovepipe brown and dry;
He wants to lay the fire himself
  with maple hard and sound,
And pop some corn upon the hearth
  when all are gathered round.
He wants the things he used to have
  when he was but a lad,
'Tis somewhat strange, it may be,
  but it makes us mightly glad;
We're both a little whiter,
  but our love, depend upon 't,
Is jest as green and stiddy
  as the hills of old Vermont.
It flustered Marm a bit at first
  about the western wife,
What she should do for one so fine
  and used to city life;
But tucked between the boy's big sheets,
  she found a little slip,
She read it with a happy tear,
  a gently quivering lip;
"Dear Mother," them's her very words,
  "I write this on the sly,
So don't tell John, but make for him
  a big, big pumpkin pie;
I know it will delight him,
  for he still is but a boy—
His mother's boy—and so he fills
  his wife's glad heart with joy."
And so, you see, 'tis busy times jest
  now for me and Marm,
The boy is comin' home to spend
  Thanksgivin' on the farm.

When Ma Is Sick

Author Unknown

When Ma is sick,
She pegs away.
She's quiet, though—
Not much to say.
She goes right on
A-doin' things,
An' sometimes laughs
Or even sings.
She says she don't
Feel extra well,
But then it's just
A kind o' spell.
She'll be all right
Tomorrow, sure;
A good old sleep
Will be the cure
An' Pa, he sniffs
An' makes no kick,
For women folks
Is always sick.
An' Ma she smiles,
Lets on she's glad.
When Ma is sick,
It ain't so bad.

BUT—

When Pa Is Sick

Author Unknown

When Pa is sick,
He's scared to death!
An' Ma an' us
Just hold our breath.
He crawls in bed
An' puffs an' grunts
An' does all kinds
Of crazy stunts.

He wants the doctor—
An' mighty quick—
For when Pa's ill,
He's awful sick.
He gasps an' groans
An' sort o' sighs.
He talks so queer,
An' rolls his eyes.

Ma jumps an' runs,
An' all of us
An' all the house
Is in a fuss.
An' peace an' joy
Is mighty skeerce.
When Pa is sick,
It's somethin' fierce!

Your Mother Still Prays for You, Jack

Author Unknown

The night was dark and stormy,
And the wind was howling wild,
When an aged mother gazed on
The portrait of her child.
As she gazed on the baby's features
That once filled her heart with joy,
He is now o'er the wide world roaming,
A mother's homeless boy.

Chorus:
Your mother still prays for you, Jack,
Your mother still prays for you,
In her home far over the ocean
Your mother still prays for you.

Far away from home and mother,
Away in this far-off land,
Some comrades said, "Come on, Jack,
There goes the army band."
It was a rough old barrack
Where the meeting had just begun,
And something touched poor Jack's heart
While sweetly the soldiers sang.

His stony heart was broken
As he thought of his mother dear,
In spite of his comrades laughing.
He could not keep from tears,
In spite of his fears of temptation.
These words in his ears still rang.
So he started for heaven that evening,
As sweetly the angels sang.

One day there came a letter,
'Twas deeply edged in black,
From a comrade long forgotten,
But he still remembered Jack.
"They have laid your dear old mother
In a grave so deep and cold,
She wants her boy that's roaming
To meet her on streets of gold."

The Mother Watch

By Edgar A. Guest

She never closed her eyes in sleep
    till we were all in bed,
On party nights till we came home
    she often sat and read,
We little thought about it then,
    when we young and gay
How much the mother worried
    when we children were away;
We only knew she never slept
    when we were out at night
And that she waited just to know
    that we'd come home all right.
Why, sometimes when we'd stayed away
    till one or two or three,
It seemed to us that Mother heard
    the turning of the key;
For always when we stepped inside
    she'd call and we'd reply.
But we were all too young back then
    to understand just why,
Until the last one had returned
    she always kept a light,
For Mother couldn't sleep until
    she'd kissed us all good night.
She had to know that we were safe
    before she went to rest,
She seemed to fear the world might harm
    the ones she loved the best.
And once she said, "When you are grown
    to women and to men,
Perhaps I'll sleep the whole night through;
    I may be different then."
And so it seemed that night and day
    we knew a mother's care,
That always when we got back home
    we'd find her waiting there.
Then came the night that we were called
    to gather round her bed.
"The children all are with you now,"
    the kindly doctor said.
And in her eyes there gleamed again
    the old-time tender light
That told she had been waiting
    just to know we were all right.
She smiled the old familiar smile
    and prayed to God to keep
Us safe from harm throughout the years
    and then she went to sleep.

Hide and Go Seek

By H.C. Bunner

It was Hide-and-Go-Seek
   they were playing,
Though you'd never have known
   it to be
With an old, old, old lady
And a boy with a twisted knee.

The boy would bend
   his face down—
On his one little sound right knee
And he'd guess where
   she was hiding,
In guesses, Onc-Two-Three!

"You are in the china closet!"
He would cry, and laugh with glee.
It wasn't the china closet;
But he still had Two and Three!

"You are up in Papa's big
   bedroom,
In the chest with the queer
   old key!"
And she said, "You are warm
   and warmer,
But you're not quite right,"
   said she.

"It can't be the little cupboard
Where Mama's things used to be
So it must be the clothes-press, Gran'ma,"
And he found her with his Three.

Then she covered her face with her fingers,
That were wrinkled and white and wee,
And she guessed where he was hiding,
With a One, and Two, and Three.

And they never had stirred from their places
Right under the maple tree—
This old, old, old lady—
And the boy with the lame little knee.
This dear, dear, dear old lady
And the boy who was half-past three.

It was an old, old, old lady—
And a boy who was half-past three
And the way they played together
Was beautiful to see.

She couldn't go running and jumping
And the boy, no more could he—
For he was a thin little fellow
With a thin little twisted knee.

They sat in the yellow sunlight,
Out under the maple tree—
And the game that they played I'll tell you,
Just as 'twas told to me.

Grandmother's Old Armchair

Author Unknown

My grandmother, she, at the age of eighty-three,
One day in May was taken ill and died;
And after she was dead, the will of course was read
By a lawyer as we all stood side by side.
To my brother, it was found, she had left a
   hundred pound,
The same unto my sister, I declare;
But when it came to me, the lawyer said, "I see
She has left to you her old armchair."

Chorus:
How they tittered, how they chaffed,
How my brother and my sisters laughed,
When they heard the lawyer declare
Granny'd only left to me her old armchair.

I thought it hardly fair, still said I did not care,
And in the evening took the chair away.
My brother at me laughed, the lawyer at me
   chaffed,
And said, "It will come useful, John, some day.
When you settle down in life,
Find some girl to be your wife,
You'll find it very handy, I declare,
On a cold and frosty night,
When the fire is burning bright,
You can sit in your old armchair."

What the lawyer said was true,
For in a year or two,
Strange to say, I settled down in married life.
I first a girl did court and then a ring I bought,
Took her to the church, and then she was my wife.
Now the dear girl and me
Are happy as can be,
And when my work is done, I declare,
I ne'er abroad would roam,
But each night I'd stay at home,
And be seated in my old armchair.

One night the chair fell down.
When I picked it up I found
The seat had fallen out upon the floor,
And there before my eyes
I saw to my surprise
A lot of notes, 10,000 pounds or more.
When my brother heard of this,
The poor fellow, I confess,
Went nearly wild with rage and tore his hair.
But I only laughed at him,
And I said unto him: "Jim,
Don't you wish you had the old armchair?"

Chorus:
No more they tittered, no more they chaffed.
No more my brother and my sisters laughed,
When they heard the lawyer declare
Granny'd only left to me her old armchair.

A Hard Day's Work

Chapter Seven

There is nothing more satisfying to me than coming to the end of the day and looking back to see the fruit of a hard day's work.

That probably comes from working the garden and fields when I was a young man. Turning to squint into the setting sun, I always took pleasure in seeing hay stacked, rows weeded or fields freed of rocks.

Work is a prevalent theme through songs and poetry of the Good Old Days, a time when folks took pride in their jobs. Be they man, woman, young or old, they all pulled their own weight, knowing the family depended upon each person helping with the load.

One such example of work-related poetry is "A Perfect Day." I've read several variations on this popular folk poem. Its picture of a hard-working farm woman shows the kind of grueling days there could be back then. With such a hard-working generation, is it any wonder that the poetry of the era often reflected A Hard Day's Work?

—*Ken Tate*

A Perfect Day

Author Unknown

Grandmother, on a winter day,
Milked the cows and fed them hay,
Slopped the hogs, saddled the mule,
And got the children off to school.
Did the washing, mopped the floors,
Washed the windows and did some chores,
Cooked a dish of home-dried fruit,
Pressed her husband's Sunday suit,
Swept the parlor, made the bed
Baked a dozen loaves of bread,
Split some firewood, and lugged it in,
Enough to fill the kitchen bin.
Cleaned the lamps and put in oil,
Stewed some apples she thought might spoil.
Churned the butter, baked a cake,
Then exclaimed, "For mercy sake,
The calves have got out of the pen!"
Went out, and chased them in again.
Gathered eggs and locked the stable,
Back to the house and set the table,
Cooked a supper that was delicious,
And afterwards washed all the dishes,
Fed the cat and sprinkled the clothes,
Mended a basket full of hose,
Then opened the organ and began to play:
"When you come to the end of a perfect day."

When Mother Cooked With Wood

By Edgar A. Guest

I do not quarrel with gas,
Our modern range is fine.
The ancient stove was doomed to pass
From Time's grim firing line.
Yet now and then there comes to me
The thought of dinners good.
And pies and cake that used to be
When Mother cooked with wood.

The ax has vanished from the yard,
The chopping block has gone.
There is no pile of cordwood hard
For boys to work upon:
There is no box that must be filled
Each morning to the hood:
Time in its ruthlessness has willed
The passing of the wood.

And yet these days were fragrant days
And spicy days and rare:
The kitchen knew a cheerful blaze
And friendliness was there.
And every appetite was keen
For breakfasts that were good
When I had scarcely turned thirteen
And Mother cooked with wood.

I used to dread my daily chore,
I used to think it tough
When Mother at the kitchen door
Said I'd not chopped enough.
And on her baking days, I know
I shirked when'er I could
And in that happy long ago
When Mother cooked with wood.

I never thought I'd wish to see
That pile of wood again;
Back then it only seemed to me
A source of pain,
And now I'd gladly give my all
To stand where once I stood,
If those rare days I could recall
When Mother cooked with wood.

When Father Shook the Stove

By Edgar A. Guest

'Twas not so many years ago,
Say, twenty-two or three,
When zero weather or below
Held many a thrill for me.
Then in my icy room I slept
A youngster's sweet repose,
And always on my form I kept
My flannel underclothes.
Then I was roused by a sudden shock,
Tho' still to sleep I strove,
I knew that it was seven o'clock
When Father shook the stove.

I never heard him quit his bed,
Or his alarm clock ring;
I never heard his gentle tread,
Or his attempt to sing;
The sun that found my windowpane
On me was wholly lost,
And tho' many a sunbeam tried in vain
To penetrate the frost.
To human voice I never stirred,
But deeper down I dove
Beneath the covers when I heard
My Father shake the stove.

Today it all comes back to me
And I can hear it still;
He seemed to take a special glee
In shaking with a will;
He flung the noisy dampers back
Then rattled steel on steel
Until the force of his attack
The building seemed to feel.
Tho' I'd a youngster's heavy eyes
All sleep from them he drove;
It seemed to me the dead must rise
When Father shook the stove.

Now radiators thump and pound,
And every room is warm,
And modern man new ways have found
To shield us from the storm.
The windowpanes are seldom glossed
The way they used to be;
The pictures left by old Jack Frost
Our children never see.
And now that he has gone to rest
In God's great slumber grove,
I often think those days were best
When Father shook the stove.

The Farmer's Boy

Author Unknown

The sun went down behind the hill,
Across the dreary moor,
When weary and lone there came a boy,
Up to the farmer's door.
"Can you tell me if any there be,
Who would me employ?
To plow, to sow, to reap and to mow,
To be a farmer's boy?

"My father is dead and my mother is left
With her five children small,
But what is worse for my mother dear
I'm the largest of them all.
Tho' little I am, I fear not work,
If you would me employ,
To plow, to sow, to reap and to mow,
And to be a farmer's boy.

"But if you have no work for me,
One favor I do ask,
Is to shelter me 'til the break of day,
From this cold wintry blast.
At the break of day, I'll travel away
Seeking for employ,
To plow, to sow, to reap and to mow,
And to be a farmer's boy."

"Let's try the lad," the farmer said.
"Let him no further seek."
"Oh, yes, dear Father!" the daughter replied,
While the tears rolled down her cheeks.
It is hard for one who would work,
Seeking for employ,
To plow, to sow, to reap and to mow,
And to be a farmer's boy.

In the course of time he grew a man,
The good old farmer died,
And left the lad the farm he had,
And his daughter for his bride.
And now, this lad a farm he had,
With many a smiling joy,
He blesses the day when he came that way
Just to be a farmer's boy.

Down on the Farm

By Harrison Flash

Down on the farm, 'bout half past four
I slip on my pants and sneak out the door
Out to the barn I run like the dickens,
To milk the cows and feed the chickens.
Clean out the barn, curry Nancy and Jiggs,
Separate the cream and feed the pigs.
Work two hours, then eat like a Turk
And by heck, I'm ready for a full day's work.

Then I grease the wagon and put on the rack,
Throw a jug of water in an old grain sack.
Hitch up the horses, hustle down the lane;
Must get the hay in, for it looks like rain.
Look over yonder, sure as I'm born,
Cattle's on the rampage and cows in the corn.
Start across the medder, run a mile or two,
Heaving like I'm windbroke,
   get wet clean through.
Get back to the horses, then for recompense
Nance gets straddle the barb wire fence.
Joints all a-aching and muscles in a jerk,
I'm fit as a fiddle for a full day's work.

Work all summer 'till winter is nigh
Then figure up the books and heave a big sigh.
Worked all year, didn't make a thing,
Got less cash now than I had last spring.
Now some people say that there ain't no hell,
But they never farmed, so how can they tell?
When spring rolls around I take another chance,
While the fringe grows longer
   on my old gray pants.
Give my s'penders a hitch, my belt another jerk,
And by heck I'm ready for a full year's work.

A Housekeeper's Tragedy

Author Unknown

One day as I wandered, I heard a complaining,
And saw a poor woman, the picture of gloom:
She glared at the mud on her doorsteps
   ('twas raining),
And this was her wail as she wielded the broom:

"Oh! life is a toil, and love is a trouble,
And beauty will fade and riches will flee;
And pleasures they dwindle,
   and prices they double,
And nothing is what I could wish it to be.

"There's too much of worriment goes to a bonnet;
There's too much of ironing goes to a shirt;
There's nothing that pays for the time
   you waste on it;
There's nothing that lasts but trouble and dirt.

"In March it is mud; it's slush in December;
The midsummer breezes are loaded with dust;
In fall the leaves litter; in muggy September
The wallpaper rots, and the candlesticks rust.

"There are worms in the cherries,
   and slugs in the roses,
And ants in the sugar and mice in the pies;
The rubbish of spiders no mortal supposes,
And ravaging roaches and damaging flies.

"It's sweeping at six, and dusting at seven;
It's victuals at eight, and dishes at nine;
It's potting and panning from ten to eleven;
We scarce break our fast ere we plan how to dine.

"With grease and with grime,
   from corner to center,
Forever at war and forever alert,
No rest for a day, lest the enemy enter—
I spend my whole life in a struggle with dirt.

"Last night, in my dreams,
   I was stationed forever,
On a bare little isle in the midst of the sea;
My one chance of life was a ceaseless endeavor,
To sweep off the waves ere they swept over me.

"Alas, 'twas no dream! Again I behold it!
I yield: I am helpless my fate to avert!"
She rolled down her sleeves,
   her apron she folded,
Then laid down and died, and was buried in dirt.

The Old Way and the New

By John H. Yates

I've just come in from the meadow, wife,
   where the grass is tall and green;
I hobbled out upon my cane
   to see John's new machine;
It made my old eyes snap again
   to see that mower mow,
And I heaved a sigh for the scythe that I swung
   some twenty years ago.

Many and many's the day I've mowed
   'neath the rays of a scorching sun,
Till I thought my poor old back would break
   ere my task for the day was done;
I often think of the days of toil
   in the fields all over the farm
Till I feel the sweat on my wrinkled brow,
   and the old pain come in my arm.

It was hard work, it was slow work,
   a-swinging the old scythe then;
Unlike the mower that went through the grass
   like death through the ranks of men.
I stood and I looked till my old eyes ached,
   amazed at its speed and power;
The work that it took me a day to do,
   it done in one short hour.

John said that I hadn't seen the half;
   when he puts it into his wheat,
I shall see it reap and rake it,
   and put it in bundles neat;
Then soon a Yankee will come along,
   and set to work and larn
To reap it, and thresh it, and bag it up,
   and send it into the barn.

John kinder laughed when he said it,
   but I said to the hired men,
"I have seen so much on my pilgrimage through
   my three score years and ten,
That I wouldn't be surprised to see
   a railroad in the air,
Or a Yankee in a flyin' ship
   a'goin' most anywhere."

There's a difference in the work I done,
   and the work my boys now do;
Steady and slow in the good old way,
   worry and fret in the new;
But somehow I think there was happiness
   crowded into those toiling days,
That the fast young men of the present
   will not see till they change their ways.

To think that I ever should live to see
   work done in this wonderful way!
Old tools are of little service now,
   and farmin' is almost play;
The women have got their sewin' machines,
   their wringers, and every sich thing,
And now they play croquet in the door-yard,
   or sit in the parlor and sing.

'Twasn't you that had it so easy, wife,
   in the days so long gone by;
You riz up early, and sat up late,
   a-toilin' for you and I.
There were cows to milk; there was butter to
   make; and many a day did you stand
A-washin' my toil-stained garments, and
   wringin' 'em out by hand.

Ah! wife, our children will never see
   the hard work we have seen,
For the heavy task and the long task is now
   done with a machine;
No longer the noise of the scythe I hear,
   the mower—there! hear it afar?
A-rattlin' along through the tall, stout grass
   with the noise of a railroad car.

Well! the old tools are all shoved away;
   they stand a-gatherin' rust
Like many an old man I have seen
   put aside with only a crust;
When the eye grows dim, when the step is weak,
   when the strength goes out of his arm,
The best thing a poor old man can do
   is to hold the deed to the farm.

There is one old way they can't improve,
  although it has been tried
By men who have studied and studied,
  and worried till they died;

It has shone undimmed for ages,
  like gold refined from its dross;
It's the way to the kingdom of heaven,
  by the simple way of the cross.

How the Churning Was Done

Author Unknown

Dear husband, I'm tired, ho, hum!
So don't leave me tonight.
But stay and make the butter come.
The cream is now just right.

But wife, as sure's
  my name is Brown,
I can't endorse your plan,
For I'm obliged to go
  downtown
Tonight to see a man.

But there's no butter
  on the shelf
For breakfast, is there, Sue?
None, so you see how
  it is yourself.
What are we, man,
  to do?

But Love, please cover
  up the churn
For just a half an hour,
And I will give the
  crank a turn
Before the cream
  can sour.

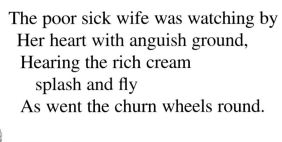

And coming back at ten o'clock
He grabbed the handle quick,
And made the butter paddles fly
Through cream, hard, thin, and thick.

The poor sick wife was watching by
  Her heart with anguish ground,
  Hearing the rich cream
    splash and fly
  As went the churn wheels round.

When for an hour he'd
  tugged and sweat,
And ready to faint, she cried.
It won't come, it's sour, I bet!
Just look dear patient saint.

He lifted the lid so careful,
  As handling silk,
  His wife had churned the cream,
    while—He had banged the
    buttermilk.

So after this affair,
  He worked a different plan.
  And always did the churning
    Before he went to see his man.

The Village Blacksmith

By Henry Wadsworth Longfellow

Under a spreading chestnut-tree
The village smithy stands;
The smith, a mighty man is he,
With large and sinewy hands;
And the muscles of his brawny arms
Are strong as iron bands.

His hair is crisp, and black, and long,
His face is like the tan;
His brow is wet with honest sweat,
He earns whate'er he can,
And looks the whole world in the face,
For he owes not any man.

Week in, week out, from morn till night,
You can hear his bellows blow;
You can hear him swing his heavy sledge
With measured beat and slow,
Like a sexton ringing the village bell,
When the evening sun is low.

The children coming home from school
Look in at the open door;
They love to see the flaming forge,
And hear the bellows roar,
And catch the burning sparks that fly
Like chaff from a threshing-floor.

He goes on Sunday to the church,
And sits among his boys;
He hears the parson pray and preach,
He hears his daughter's voice,
Singing in the village choir,
And it makes his heart rejoice.

It sounds to him like his mother's voice,
Singing in Paradise!
He needs must think of her once more,
How in the grave she lies;
And with his hard, rough hand he wipes
A tear out of his eyes.

Toiling,—rejoicing,—sorrowing,
Onward through life he goes;
Each morning sees some task begun,
Each evening sees it close;
Something attempted, something done,
Has earned a night's repose.

Thanks, thanks to thee,
    my worthy friend,
For the lesson thou hast
    taught!
Thus at the flaming forge
    of life
Our fortunes must be
    wrought;
Thus on its sounding
    anvil shaped
Each burning deed and
    thought!

Kraut-Makin' Time

Author Unknown

When I wuz just a kid at home
I'd watch Grandma move about
And I could tell every time
When she planned on makin' kraut.
She'd go down in the cellar
And bring up a great big crock
Then out to the rock pile
To find the biggest rock.

She'd wash and scrub the whole "she-bang"
'Till it was sparkling clean;
The old kraut cutter and big dishpan
Were next upon the scene.
Then she gathered in the cabbage.
The big heads and the small,
She never threw a head away
If it could be used at all.

She'd trim the outer leaves away
'Till it was pearly white
Then she started cutting it
My what a welcomed sight!
And when the dishpan got so full
She'd salt and mix it good
Then dump it in the crock
    and stamp it
With a gadget made of
    wood.

And when the juice
    came oozing up
I'd have to have a taste
Then watch Grandma
    put in "hearts"—
Even those, she didn't
    waste.
With every batch
    she'd dump in
A taste I'd have to take;
Don't know why
    I didn't get
An awful stomachache.

The cabbage was covered with
    a clean white cloth
There in that precious crock
Then a plate, turned upside down,
Was weighted down by the rock.
Another cloth she'd cover all
And set it to one side
Then in a few days, you'd vow
Something had crawled in and died.

And if folks happened in
You was so embarrassed by the smell
And you'd start explaining
And hoped you'd do it well.
This one question I've tried to answer
But somehow I never could:
"How can anything smell so bad
Yet taste so awful good?"

When the Work's All Done This Fall

Author Unknown

A group of jolly cowboys,
  discussing plans at ease,
Says one: "I'll tell you something, boys,
  if you will listen, please.
I am an old cow-puncher,
  and here I'm dressed in rags.
I used to be a tough one
  and go on great big jags.
But I have got a home, boys,
  a good one, you all know,
Although I have not seen it
  since long, long ago.
I'm going back to Dixie
  once more to see them all.
I'm going to see my mother
when the work's all done this fall.

"After the roundup's over
  and after the shipping's done,
I'm going right straight home, boys,
  ere all my money's gone.
I have changed my ways, boys,
  no more will I fall;
And I am going home to Mother,
When the work's all done this fall.
"When I left my home, boys,
  my mother for me cried,
Begged me not to leave her;
  for me she would have died;
My mother's heart is breaking,
  breaking for me, boys, that's all,
And with God's help I'll see her
when the work's all done this fall."

That very night this cowboy
  went out to stand his guard;
The night was dark and cloudy
  and storming very hard.
The cattle they got frightened
  and rushed in wild stampede.
The cowboy tried to head them,
  while riding at full speed.

While riding in the darkness,
  so loudly did he shout,
Trying his best to head them
  and turn the herd about,
His saddle horse did stumble,
  and on him it did fall.
The boy won't see his mother
when the work's all done this fall.

His body was so mangled
  the boys all thought him dead.
They picked him up so gently
  and laid him on a bed.
He opened wide his blue eyes
  and looking all around,
He motioned to his comrades
  to come sit near him on the ground.
"Boys, send my mother my wages,
  the wages I have earned,
For I am afraid boys,
  my last steer I have turned.
I'm going to a new range;
  I hear my Master's call,
And I'll not see my mother
when the work's all done this fall.

"Bill, you take my saddle;
  George, you take my bed;
Jack, you take my pistol,
  after I am dead.
Boys, think of me kindly
  when you look upon them all,
For I'll not see my mother
when the work's all done this fall."
Poor Charley was buried at sunrise,
  no tombstone at his head,
Nothing but a little board;
  and this is what it said:
"Charley died at daybreak;
  he died from a fall.
The boy won't see his mother
when the work's all done this fall."

Love of Country

Chapter Eight

The selection of poems and songs for this chapter was a formidable task. There have been so many patriotic verses penned that I didn't know quite where to start.

I then remembered an old war song I learned as a child. "Tenting on the Old Camp Ground" carried such a haunting melody that it became a favorite of mine. Its message of war-weary soldiers fighting for peace conveyed the message so many of us felt: We hated war, but we loved freedom and justice, not just for us but for all mankind.

In those Good Old Days of the early part of the 20th Century, we still had Civil War veterans visiting schools on patriotic holidays. Before and after World War II, they were replaced by dough boys from "The Great War." Today, our fighting men from World War II are seeing their ranks thinned daily.

This chapter is dedicated to all those who stood up, braving the ultimate sacrifice to serve God and country in the dark days of war. Their actions—and these verses—reflect their great Love of Country.

—Ken Tate

Tenting on the Old Camp Ground

By W. Kittredge

We're tenting tonight
On the old camp ground,
Give us a song to cheer
Our weary hearts,
A song of home
And friends we love so dear.

Chorus:
Many are the hearts that are weary tonight,
Wishing for the war to cease;
Many are the hearts looking for the right
To see the dawn of peace.
Tenting tonight, tenting tonight,
Tenting on the old camp ground.

We've been tenting tonight
On the old camp ground,
Thinking of days gone by,

Of the lov'd ones at home
That gave us the hand,
And the tear that said "Goodbye."

We are tired of war
On the old camp ground,
Many are dead and gone,
Of the brave and true
Who've left their homes,
Others been wounded long.

We've been fighting today
On the old camp ground,
Many are lying near;
Some are dead
And some are dying,
Many are in tears.

The Flag Is Passing By

By Henry Holcomb Bennett

Hats off!

Along the street there comes
A blare of bugles, a ruffle of drums,
A flash of color beneath the sky:

Hats off!

The flag is passing by!
Blue and crimson and white it shines,
Over the steel-tipped, ordered lines:

Hats off!

The colors before us fly.
But more than the flag is
    passing by,
Sea-fights and land-fights,
Grim and great,
Fought to make
And to save the State;
Weary marches
And sinking ships,
Cheers of victory
On dying lips;
Days of plenty
And years of peace;
March of a strong land's
Swift increase;
Equal justice,
Right and law,
Stately honor
And reverent awe.
Sign of a nation
Great and strong
To ward her people
From foreign wrong;
Pride and glory
And honor—all
Live in the colors
To stand or fall.

Hats off!

Along the street there comes
A blare of bugles, a ruffle of drums;
And loyal hearts are beating high:

Hats off!

The flag is passing by!

I Am Your Flag

By Thomas E. Wicks, Sr.

I AM YOUR FLAG.
I was born June 14, 1777.
I am more than just cloth shaped into a design.
I am the refuge
of the world's oppressed people.
I am the silent sentinel of Freedom.
I am the emblem
of the greatest sovereign nation on earth.
I am the inspiration
for which American Patriots
gave their lives and fortunes.
I have led your sons into battle
from Valley Forge
to the bloody ridges of Korea.
I walk in silence
with each of your Honored Dead
to their final resting place
beneath the silent white crosses,
row upon row.
I have flown through peace and war,
Strife and prosperity,
And amidst it all, I have been respected.

I AM YOUR FLAG.
My Red Stripes
symbolize the blood spilled
in defense of this Glorious Nation.
My White Stripes

signify the burning tears
shed by Americans who lost their sons.
My Blue Field
is indicative of God's heaven,
under which I fly.
My stars, clustered together,
unify 50 states as one,
for God and Country.
"Old Glory" is my nickname,
and proudly I wave on high.
Honor me, respect me, defend me
with your lives
and your fortunes.
Never let my enemies tear me down
from my lofty position,
lest I never return.
Keep alight
the fires of patriotism,
Strive earnestly
for the spirit of democracy.
Worship Eternal God,
and keep His Commandments,
And I shall remain the bulwark
of peace
and freedom
for all mankind.

I AM YOUR FLAG.

John
Slobodnik

Just a Common Soldier

Author Unknown

He was getting old and paunchy
And his hair was falling fast
And he sat around the Legion
Telling stories of the past.
Of a war that he had fought in
And the deeds that he had done.
In his exploits with his buddies
They were heroes every one.

Tho' sometimes to his neighbors,
His tales became a joke,
All his Legion buddies listened
For they knew whereof he spoke.
But we'll hear his tales no longer,
For old Bill has passed away,
And the world's a little poorer
For a soldier died today.

He'll not be mourned by many,
Just his children and his wife.
For he lived an ordinary
Quiet and uneventful life.
Held a job and raised a family,
Quietly going his own way;
And the world won't note his passing,
Though a soldier died today.

When politicians leave this earth
Their bodies lie in state,
While thousands note their passing
And proclaim they were great,
Papers tell their life stories from
The time they were young.
But the passing of a soldier
Goes unnoticed and unsung.

Is the greatest contribution
To the welfare of our land
A guy who breaks his promises
And cons his fellow man?
Or the ordinary fellow who
In times of war and strife
Goes off to serve his country
And offers up his life?

A politician's stipend and the
Style in which he lives
Are sometimes disproportionate
To the service that he gives
While the ordinary soldier
Who offers his all
Is paid off with a medal
And perhaps a pension small.

It's so easy to forget them,
For it was so long ago
That the "Old Bills" of our country
Went to battle, but we know
It was not the politicians
With the compromise and ploys
Who won for us the freedom
That our country now enjoys.

Should you find yourself in danger
With your enemies at hand
Would you want a politician
With his ever shifting stand?
Or would you prefer a soldier
Who has sworn to defend
His home, his kin and country
And would fight until the end?

He was just a common soldier
And his ranks are growing thin
And his presence should remind us
We may need his like again
For when countries are in conflict
Then we find the soldier's part
Is to clean up troubles
That politicians start.

If we cannot do him honour
While he's here to hear the praise
Then at least let's give him homage
At the ending of his days,
Perhaps just a simple headline
In a paper that would say:
"Our country is in Mourning
For a soldier died today."

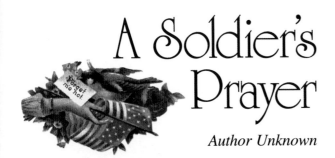

A Soldier's Prayer

Author Unknown

Tall and straight he bore his weapon
With his boots in steady beat,
Stepping proudly with his unit
Down the sunlit city street.
Brave lad chanting with the footsteps,
Neither looking left or right,
Following the Nation's banner
Straight into the endless fight.

To a land of strife and battle
Far across the wide blue sea
He has gone to help the people
Who are struggling to be free.
In the sultry heat of the swampland
In the insect-ridden mire
He has grown as tough as leather
And his heart is full of fire.

Now he sees his buddies falling
One by one they meet their doom;
While the rockets light the Heavens
Sadness shrouds his heart with gloom.
Like an old man bent and weary
In the muddy foxhole there
Knelt the lad in noise of battle
As he offered up a prayer.

"Heavenly Father, hear your child:
Why must people suffer so?
I'm so weary of this battle …
Surely, Father, you must know.
In your gentle way bring comfort
To my buddies lying there,
Ease their pain with all your mercy.
This, dear Father, is my prayer."

Then he raised his eyes to Heaven
And a teardrop softly fell
As he mourned for all who suffer
In that burning battle hell.
As he rose to struggle onward
Silhouette against the sky,
One lone sniper raised his rifle
And 'twas heard a pleading cry.

Oh so young to die in battle
Far from loved ones all alone;
His still face was turned to Heaven
Waiting for his journey home.

In Flanders Fields the Poppies Grow

By Major John D. McCrae

In Flanders fields the poppies blow
Between the crosses, row on row,
That mark our place; and in the sky
The larks, still bravely singing, fly,
Scarce heard amid the guns below.

We are the Dead. Short days ago
We lived, felt dawn, saw sunset glow,
Loved and were loved, and now we lie
    In Flanders fields.

Take up our quarrel with the foe!
To you from failing hands, we throw
The torch—Be yours to hold it high!
If ye break faith with us who die
We shall not sleep,
    though poppies grow
In Flanders fields.

The Unknown Soldier

By Billy Rose

There's a graveyard near the White House
Where the Unknown Soldier lies,
And the flowers there are sprinkled
With the tears from
	mothers' eyes.

I stood there not so
	long ago
With roses for the
	brave,
And suddenly I
	heard a voice
Speak from the
	grave:

"I am the Unknown
	Soldier,"
The spirit voice
	began,
"And I think I have
	the right to ask
Some questions,
	man to man.

"Are my buddies
	taken care of?
Was their victory
	so sweet?
Is that big reward you offered
Selling pencils on the street?

"Did they really win the freedom
They battled to achieve?
Do you still respect the Croix de Guerre
Above that empty sleeve?

"Does a Gold Star in the window
Now mean anything at all?
I wonder how my old girl feels
		When she hears
		the bugle call?

"And that baby
	who sang
'Hello, Central,
	give me No
	Man's Land,'
Can they replace
	her daddy
With a military
	band?

"I wonder if the
	profiteers
Have sacrificed
	their greed?
I wonder if a
	soldier's mother
Ever is in need?

"I wonder if the
	kings who
	planned it all
Are really satisfied?
They played their game of checkers
And eleven million died.

"I am the Unknown Soldier,
And maybe died in vain,
But if I were alive and my country called,
I'd do it all over again."

Paul Revere's Ride *By Henry Wadsworth Longfellow*

Listen, my children, and you shall hear
Of the midnight ride of Paul Revere,
On the eighteenth of April, in Seventy-five;
Hardly a man is now alive
Who remembers that famous day and year.

He said to his friend, "If the British march
By land or sea from the town tonight,
Hang a lantern aloft in the belfry arch
Of the North Church tower as a signal light,—

One, if by land, and two, if by sea;
And I on the opposite shore will be,
Ready to ride
    and spread the alarm
Through every Middlesex
    village and farm,
For the country folk to be
    up and to arm."

Then he said, "Good night!"
    and with muffled oar
Silently rowed to the
    Charlestown shore,
Just as the moon rose
    over the bay,
Where swinging wide
    at her moorings lay
The Somerset, British
    man-of-war;
A phantom ship, with each mast and spar
Across the moon like a prison bar,
And a huge black hulk, that was magnified
By its own reflection in the tide.

Meanwhile, his friend, through alley and street,
Wanders and watches with eager ears,
Till in the silence around him he hears
The muster of men at the barrack door,
The sound of arms, and the tramp of feet
And the measured tread of the grenadiers,
Marching down to their boats on the shore.

Then he climbed the tower
    of the Old North Church,
By the wooden stairs, with stealthy tread,
To the belfry-chamber overhead,

And startled the pigeons from their perch
On the somber rafters, that round him made
Masses and moving shapes of shade,—
By the trembling ladder, steep and tall,
To the highest window in the wall,
Where he paused to listen and look down
A moment on the roofs of the town,
And the moonlight flowing over all.

Beneath, in the churchyard, lay the dead,
In their night encampment on the hill,
Wrapped in silence so deep and still
That he could hear, like a sentinel's tread,
The watchful night-wind,
    as it went
Creeping along from tent to tent,
And seeming to whisper,
    "All is well!"
A moment only he feels the spell
Of the place and the hour,
    and the secret dread
Of the lonely belfry
    and the dead;
For suddenly all his thoughts
    are bent
On a shadowy something
    far away,
Where the river widens
    to meet the bay,—
A line of black
    that bends and floats
On the rising tide, like a bridge of boats.

Meanwhile, impatient to mount and ride,
Booted and spurred, with a heavy stride
On the opposite shore walked Paul Revere.
Now he patted his horse's side,
Now gazed at the landscape far and near,
Then, impetuous, stamped the earth,
And turned and tightened his saddle girth;
But mostly he watched with eager search
The belfry-tower of the Old North Church,
As it rose above the graves on the hill,
Lonely and spectral and somber and still.
And lo! as he looks, on the belfry's height
A glimmer, and then a gleam of light!
He springs to the saddle, the bridle he turns,

But lingers and gazes, till fall on his sight
A second lamp in the belfry burns!

A hurry of hoofs in a village street,
A shape in the moonlight, a bulk in the dark,
And beneath, from the pebbles,
    in passing, a spark
Struck out by a steed flying fearless and fleet;
That was all! And yet, through the gloom
    and the light
The fate of a nation was riding that night;
And the spark struck out by that steed
    in his flight,
Kindled the land into flame with its heat.

He has left the village and mounted the steep,
And beneath him, tranquil and broad and deep,
Is the Mystic, meeting the ocean tides;
And under the alders, that skirt its edge,
Now soft on the sand, now loud on the ledge,
Is heard the tramp of his steed as he rides.

It was twelve by the village clock
When he crossed the bridge into Medford town.
He heard the crowing of the cock,
And the barking of the farmer's dog,
And felt the damp of the river fog,
That rises after the sun goes down.

It was one by the village clock,
When he galloped into Lexington.
He saw the gilded weathercock
Swim in the moonlight as he passed,
And the meeting-house windows, blank and bare,
Gaze at him with a spectral glare,
As if they already stood aghast
At the bloody work they would look upon.

It was two by the village clock,
When he came to the bridge in Concord town.
He heard the bleating of the flock,
And the twitter of birds among the trees,
And felt the breath of the morning breeze
Blowing over the meadows brown.
And one was safe and asleep in his bed
Who at the bridge would be first to fall,
Who that day would be lying dead,
Pierced by a British musket-ball.

You know the rest. In the books you have read,
How the British Regulars fired and fled,—
How the farmers gave them ball for ball,
From behind each fence and farmyard wall,
Chasing the redcoats down the lane,
Then crossing the fields to emerge again
Under the trees at the tarn of the road,
And only pausing to fire and load.

So through the night
    rode Paul
    Revere;
And so through
    the night went
    his cry of alarm
To every
    Middlesex
    village and
    farm,—
A cry of
    defiance,
    and not of
    fear,
A voice in the
    darkness, a
    knock at the
    door,
And a word that
    shall echo
    forevermore!
For, borne on
    the night-
    wind of the
    Past,
Through all
    our history,
    to the last,
In the hour of
    darkness and
    peril and
    need,
The people will
    waken and
    listen to hear
The hurrying hoofbeats
    of that steed,
And the midnight message
    of Paul Revere.

The Ride of Jennie McNeal

By Will Carleton

Paul Revere was a rider bold—
Well has his valorous deed been told;
Sheridan's ride was a glorious one—
Often it has been dwelt upon.
But why should men do all the deeds
On which the love of a patriot feeds?
Harken to me, while I reveal
The dashing ride of Jennie McNeal.

On a spot as pretty as might be found
In the dangerous length of the Neutral Ground,
In a cottage cozy,
   and all their own,
She and her mother
   lived alone.
Safe were the two,
   with their frugal
   store,
From all of the
   many who passed
   their door;
For Jennie's mother
   was strange to fears
And Jennie was large for
   fifteen years:

With fun her eyes here glistening,
Her hair was the hue of blackbird's wing,
And while the friends who knew her well
The sweetness of her heart could tell;
A gun that hung on the kitchen wall
Looked solemnly quick to heed her call;
And they who were evil-minded knew
Her nerve was strong and her aim was true,
So all kind words and acts did deal
To generous black-eyed Jennie McNeal.

One night when the sun had crept to bed,
And rain clouds lingered overhead
And sent their pearly drops for proof
To drum a tune on the cottage roof,
Close after a knock at the outer door,

There entered a dozen dragoons or more,
Their red coats, stained by the muddy road,
That they were British soldiers showed;
The captain his hostess bent to greet,
Saying, "Madam, please give us a bite to eat;
We will pay you well, and it may be,
This bright-eyed girl, for pouring our tea.
"Then we must dash ten miles ahead
To catch a rebel colonel abed.
He is visiting home, as doth appear;
We will make his pleasure cost him dear."
   And they fell on the hasty supper
     with zeal,
     Close watched the while by
     Jennie McNeal,

     For the gray-haired
      colonel that
      hovered near
     Had been her true
      friend—kind and dear,
     And told her stories,
      many a one,
     Concerning the French Wall
    lately done.
And oft together the two friends were,
And many the arts he had taught to her;
She had hunted by his fatherly side—
He had shown her how to fence and ride,
And once had said, "The time may be
Your skill and courage may stand by me."
So sorrow for him she could but feel,
Brave, grateful-hearted Jennie McNeal.

With never a thought or a moment more,
Bare-headed she slipped from the cottage door;
Ran out where the horses were left to feed
Unhitched and mounted the captain's steed,
And down the hilly and rock-strewn way
She urged the fiery horse of gray.
Around her slender and cloakless form
Pattered and moaned the ceaseless storm;

Secure and tight, a gloveless hand
Grasped the reins with a stern command;
And full and black her long hair streamed
Whenever the ragged lightning gleamed.
And on she rushed for the colonel's weal,
Brave, lioness-hearted Jennie McNeal.

Hark—from the hills a moment mute,
Came a clatter of hoofs in hot pursuit;
And a cry from the foremost trooper said:
"Halt, or your blood be on your head!"
She heeded it not; not in vain
She lashed the horse, with the bridle rein.
So into the night the gray horse strode;
His shoes heaved fire from the rocky road
And the high-born courage that never dies
Flashed from the rider's coal-black eyes.
The pebbles flew from the fearful race,
The raindrops splashed on her glowing face,
"On, on brave beast," with loud appeal
Cried eager, resolute Jennie McNeal.

"Halt!" once more came the voice of dread,
"Halt, or your blood be on your head!"
Then, no one answering to the calls,
Shed after her a volley of balls.
They screamed to her left,
    they screamed to her right,
She sent no token of answer back
Except a silvery laughter peal,
Brave, merry-hearted Jennie McNeal.

So on she rushed at her own good will.
Through wood and valley, o'er plain and hill;
The gray horse did his duty well,
Till all at once he stumbled and fell,
Himself escaping the nets of harm,
But flinging the girl, with a broken arm;
Still undismayed by the numbing pain
She clung to the horse's bridle rein,
And gently bidding him to stand
She sprang again to the saddle bow,
And shouted, "One more trial now!"
As if ashamed of the heedless fall,
He gathered his strength once more for all,

And galloping down a hillside steep,
Gained on the troopers at every leap.
No more the high-bred steed did reel,
But ran his best for Jennie McNeal.

They were a furlong behind, or more,
When the girl burst through the colonel's door.
Her poor arm helpless, hanging with pain,
And she all drabbled and drenched with rain
But her cheeks as red as firebrands are,
And her eyes as bright as a blazing star.
She shouted, "Quick! Be quick, I say!
The come! They come! Away! Away!"
Then sunk on the rude white floor of deal,
Poor brave, exhausted Jennie McNeal.

The startled Colonel sprang and pressed
His wife and children to his breast,
Then turned away from the fireside bright
And glided into the stormy night.
He soon and safely made his way
To where the patriot army lay;
But first he bent in the dim firelight
And kissed the forehead broad and white
And blessed the girl who had ridden so well
To keep him out of a prison cell.
The girl roused up at the martial din
Just as the trooper came rushing in,
And laughed, e'en in the midst of a groan,
Saying, "Good sires, your bird has flown.
'Tis I who have scared him from his nest,
So deal with me now as you think best."

But the bold young captain bowed and said:
"Never you hold a moment's dread,
Of womankind I must crown you Queen;
So brave a girl I have never seen;
Wear this gold ring as your valor's due
And when peace comes, I will come for you."
But Jennie's face an arch smile wore
As she said, "There's a lad in Putnam's Corps
Who told me the same long time ago;
You two would never agree, I know;
I promised my love to be true as steel,"
Said good, sure-hearted Jennie McNeal.

Land Poetic

Author Unknown

I've traveled the U.S. highways
A million miles and more
From the majestic Pacific mountains
To the tranquil Eastern Shore.

I've seen the lakes and rivers wide,
The mountain rills and streams,
The flowers wild by the countryside,
A beauty beyond my dreams.

I've seen the plains in the great Midwest,
The tumbleweeds and thistles,
The deserts bare with beauty rare
And heard the Eastbound's whistles.

I've heard the call of the meadowlark
And seen the brown trout running,
I've seen the coyote, heard his bark,
And watched the bathers sunning.

I've seen amigos in the shade
And quaint adobe huts
And all the refreshing verdant glades
And dried-up creekbed ruts.

I've seen the redwoods great and tall,
The beauteous rocks and caverns
And heard the wild dove's mating call
And the singing in the taverns.

I've seen the mountains
    capped with snow,
The Black Hills of South Dakota,

And felt the sting of the winds that blow
In Maine and Minnesota.

I've watched the cowpokes round 'em up
On the widespread open ranches,
Drunk coffee from a campfire cup,
Smoked a peace pipe with Comanches.

I've seen canals and locks
And inland waterways,
Fishing piers and docks
And spacious coves and bays.

I've watched the motorboats at play,
Seen riverboats and barges,
The placid lakes and rattlesnakes
And grand canyons and gorges.

I've seen the many Army camps
Defending our great nation,
Skyscrapers tall tow'ring over all
And a movie on location.

Then on a Sunday morningtide
I've seen the church's steeple
And the wooden pews inside
Filled with thankful people.

In this great land we have it all;
There's nothing that we miss.
Let's thank the Lord that we've been born
To live in a land like this!
Amen!

Faith & Inspiration

Chapter Nine

s a lay preacher for over a quarter of a century, I often turned to poets for inspiration. They often gave me a fresh angle on a sermon topic, or at least a catchy introduction.

It's fitting that the final chapter in this book of *Mother's Favorite Verses* should be poetry devoted to the spiritual side of life. For many mothers—and fathers, too, for that matter—spiritual poems and songs were the favorite of their favorites.

This chapter of some of the most requested verse of the Good Old Days will remind you of why those days were filled with Faith and Inspiration.

—Ken Tate

When the Chickens Come Home to Roost

Author Unknown

You may take the world as it comes and goes,
And you'll be sure to find
That God will square
   the account he owes,
Whosoever comes out behind.
And all the things wrong
   that a man has done,
By whatever induced,
Will drift back to meet him
   face to face,
When the chickens
   come home to roost.

You may scrape and toil
   and pinch and save,
While your hoarded wealth
   expands,
'Til the cold dark shadow of the grave
Is nearing your life's last stand.
But you'll have your balance struck some night,
And you'll find your hoard reduced,
And you'll view your life in another light,
When the chickens come home to roost.

Sow as you will, there's a time to reap,
   For the good and bad as well;
   And conscience, whether we
     wake or sleep,
   Is either a heaven or a hell.
   But every wrong
     will find its place,
   And every passion loosed
   Will drift back to meet
     you face to face,
   When the chickens come
     home to roost.

   Whether you're over
     or under the sod
   The result will be the same;
   You cannot escape
     the hand of God,
   You must bear your sin and shame;
No matter what's carved on a marble slab,
When the items are all produced
You'll find that God was keeping tab,
When the chickens come home to roost.

The Model Church

Author Unknown

Well, wife, I've found the model church,
And worshipped there today;
It made me think of good old times,
Before my hair was grey;
The meeting house was finer built
Than they were years ago;
But then I found, when I went in,
It was not built for show.

The sexton did not set me down
Away back by the door;
He knew that I was old and deaf
And saw that I was poor;
He must have been a Christian man—
He led me boldly through
The crowded aisle of that grand church,
To find a pleasant pew.

I wish you'd heard the singing, wife;
It had the old-time ring;
The preacher said, with trumpet voice,
"Let all the people sing!"
"All hail the power!" was the hymn;
The music upward rolled,
Until I thought the angel choir
Struck all their harps of gold.

My deafness seemed to melt away,
My spirit caught the fire;
I joined my feeble, trembling voice,
With that melodious choir;
And sang, as in my youthful days,
"Let angels prostrate fall!
Bring forth the royal diadem,
And crown Him, crown Him,
    crown Him Lord of all!"

I tell you, wife, it did me good
To sing that hymn once more;
I felt like some wrecked mariner
Who gets a glimpse of shore.
I almost want to lay aside
This weather-beaten form,
And anchor in the blessed port,
Forever from the storm.

'Twas not a flowery sermon, wife,
But simple Gospel truth!
It fitted humble men like me;
It suited hopeful youth,
To win immortal souls to Christ
The earnest preacher tried;
He talked not of himself, or creed,
But Jesus crucified!

Dear wife, the toil will soon be o'er,
The victory soon be won;
The shining land is just ahead,
Our race is nearly run;
We're nearing Canaan's happy shore,
Our home so bright and fair;
Thank God, we'll never sin again:
"There'll be no sorrow
    there!
There'll be no
    sorrow there!
In heaven above,
    where all is
    love,
There'll be no
    sorrow
    there!"

The Deck of Cards

Author Unknown

During the North African campaign, a bunch of soldier boys had been on a long hike. They arrived in a little town called Cassino, and the next day being Sunday, several of the boys went to church.

After the chaplain read the prayer, the text was taken up. Those of the boys who had prayer books read them out, but one boy had only a deck of cards, so he spread them out.

The sergeant who commanded the boys saw the cards and said, "Soldier, put away those cards."

After the service was over, the soldier was taken prisoner and brought before the provost marshal. The provost marshal said, "Sergeant, why have you brought this man here?"

"For playing cards in church, sir."

"And what have you to say for yourself, son?"

"Much, sir," the soldier replied.

The marshal said, "I hope so, for if not, I shall punish you severely."

The soldier said, "You see, sir, I have been on the march for six days and I had neither Bible nor prayer book, but I hope to satisfy you, sir, with the purity of my intentions.

"You see, sir, when I look at the ace, it reminds me there is but one God, and when I see the deuce, it reminds me that the Bible is divided into two parts, the old and new testaments.

"And when I see the trey, I think of the Father, the Son and the Holy Ghost.

"And when I see the four, I think of the four evangelists who preached the gospel. The were Matthew, Mark, Luke and John.

"And when I see the five, it reminds me of the five virgins who trimmed their lamps. There were ten of them—five were wise and were saved; five were foolish and were shut out.

"And when I see the six, it reminds me that in six days, God made this great heaven and earth.

"And when I see the seven, it reminds me that on the seventh day, God rested.

"When I see the eight, I think of the eight righteous persons God saved when He destroyed this Earth. These were Noah, his wife, their three sons and their wives.

"When I see the nine, I think of the lepers our Savior cleansed and nine of the ten didn't even thank Him.

"When I see the ten, I think of the ten commandments God handed to Moses on the tablet of stone.

"And when I see the King, it reminds me once again there is but one King of Heaven, God Almighty.

"And when I see the queen, I think of the blessed Virgin Mary, who is Queen of Heaven.

"And the Jack or knave is the devil.

"When I count the number of spots on a deck of cards, I find 365, the number of days in a year. There are 52 cards, the number of weeks in a year. There are 13 tricks, the number of weeks in a quarter. There are four suits, the number of weeks in a month. There are 12 picture cards, the number of months in a year.

"So you see, sir, my deck of cards has served me as a Bible, almanac and prayer book."

And, friends, this story is true. I know, because I was that soldier.

My Mother's Bible

By George P. Morris

This book is all that's left me now,
Tears will forbidden start—
With faltering lip and throbbing brow
I press it to my heart.
For many generations past,
Here is our family tree;
My mother's hand this Bible clasped;
She, dying, gave it to me.

Ah, well do I remember those
Whose names these records bear,
Who round the hearthstone used to close
After the evening prayer,
And speak of what these pages said,
In tones my heart would thrill!
Though they are with the silent dead,
Here they are living still!

My father read this Holy Book
To brothers, sisters, dear;
How calm was my poor mother's look,
Who leaned, God's word to hear.
Her angel face—I see it yet!
What thronging memories come!
Again that little group is met
Within the halls of home!

Thou truest friend man ever knew,
Thy constancy I've tried;
When all were false I found thee true,
My counselor and guide.
The mines of earth no treasure give
That could this volume buy;
In teaching me the way to live
It taught me how to die.

If Jesus Came to Your House

Author Unknown

If Jesus came to your house
To spend a day or two,
If He came unexpectedly
I wonder what you'd do?

Oh, I know you'd give your nicest room
To such an honored guest
And all the food you'd serve Him
Would be the very best.

And you would keep
    assuring Him
You're glad to have Him
    there;
That serving Him
    in your home
Was joy beyond
    compare.

But when you saw
    Him coming,
Would you meet Him
    at the door,
Showing Him He's the
    one you seek
To worship and adore?

Or would you have to
    change your clothes
Before you let Him in,
And hide some magazines and put
The Bibles where they'd been?

Would you turn off the radio
And hope He hadn't heard
And wish you hadn't uttered
That last loud nasty word?

Would you hide your worldly music
And put some hymn books out?
Could you let Jesus walk right in
Or would you rush about?

And I wonder if the Savior
Spent a day or two with you,

Would you go right on doing
The things you always do?

Would you go right on saying
The things you always say?
Would life for you continue
As it does from day to day?

Would the family conversation
Keep at its usual pace?
And would you find it
hard each meal
To say a table grace?

Would you sing the songs
you've always sung
And read the books
you've read?
And let the Savior know
the things
On which your mind
and spirit fed?

Would you take Jesus
with you
Everywhere you'd planned
to go?
Or would you maybe
change your plans
For just a day or so?

Would you be glad to have Him stay
Forever, on and on?
Or would you sigh with great relief
When He at last was gone?

Would you be glad to have Him meet
Your very closest friends?
Or would you hope they'd stay away
Until His visit ends?

It might be interesting to know
The things that you would do
If Jesus came to your house
To spend a day or two.

The Good Teacher

By Henry van Dyke

The Lord is my teacher,
I shall not lose my way;
He leadeth me
In lowly paths of learning,
He prepareth a lesson for me
Every day;
He bringeth me
To the clear fountains of instructions,
Little by little
He showeth me the beauty of truth.

The world is a great book
That He hath written,
He turneth the leaves for me
Slowly;
They are all inscribed
With images and letters,
He poureth light
On the pictures and the words.

He taketh me by the hand
To the hilltop of vision,
And my soul is glad
When I perceive His meaning;
In the valley also
He walketh beside me,
In the dark places
He whispered to my heart.

Even though my lesson be hard,
It is not hopeless,
For the Lord is patient
With His slow scholar;
He will wait awhile
For my weakness,
And help me
To read the truth through tears.

It Will Show

Author Unknown

You don't have to tell
How you live every day,
You need not reveal
If you work or play;
For a trusty barometer's
Always in place—
However you live
It will show in your face.

The truth or deceit
You would hide in your heart
They will not stay inside
When once given a start;
Sinews and blood are like
Thin veils of lace—
What you wear in your heart
You must wear on your face.

If you've battled and won
In the great game of life,
If you've striven and conquered
Through sorrows and strife,
If you've played the game fair
But reached only first base,
No need to proclaim it—
It shows on your face.

My Angels

Translated from the German by Rev. G. Jaegen

At evening when I go to rest,
Fourteen angels I request.
Two to guard above my head;
Two to watch below my bed;
Two to be at my right side;
At my left two more abide;
Two to lull me into sleep;
Two to wake me from the deep;
Two to lead me on the way
Where angels always sing and pray.

The Preacher's Vacation

Author Unknown

The old man went to meeting,
For the day was bright and fair,
Though his limbs were very tottering
And 'twas hard to travel there;
But he hungered for the Gospel
As he trudged the weary way,
In the road so rough and dusty
'Neath the summer's burning ray.

By and by he reached the building,
To a soul a holy place.
Then he paused and wiped the sweat dry
Off his thin and wrinkled face;
But he looked around bewildered,
For the old bell did not toll,
And the doors were shut and bolted
And he did not see a soul.

So he leaned upon his crutches,
And he said, "What does it mean?"
And he looked this way and that
Till it seemed almost a dream;
He had walked the dusty highway—
And he breathed a heavy sigh—
Just to go once more to meetin'
Ere the summons came to die.

But he saw a little notice
Tacked upon the meetin' door,
So he limped along to read it,
And he read it o'er and o'er;
Then he wiped his dusty glasses
And read it o'er again,
Till his limbs began to tremble
And his eyes began to pain.

As the old man read the notice,
How it made his spirit burn!
"Pastor absent on vacation,
Church is closed till his return."
Then he staggered slowly backward,
And sat him down to think,
For his soul was stirred within him
Till he thought his heart would sink.

So he mused along and wondered,
To himself soliloquized:
"I've lived till almost eighty,
And was never so surprised
As I read that oddest notice
Sticking on the meetin' door,
'Pastor on vacation,'
Never heard the like before.

"Why, when I first joined the meetin'
Very many years ago,
Preachers traveled on the circuit
In the heat and through the snow;
If they got their clothes and victuals
('Twas but little cash they got),
They said nothing 'bout vacation,
But were happy in their lot.

"Would the farmer leave his cattle,
Or the shepherd leave his sheep?
Who would give them care and shelter
Or provide them food to eat?
So it strikes me very sing'lar
When a man of holy hands
Thinks he needs to have vacation
And forsake his tender lambs.

"Did St. Paul get such a notion?
Did a Wesley, or a Knox?
Did they in the heat of summer
Turn away their needy flocks?
Did they shut their meetin' house,
Just to go and lounge about?
Why, they knew that if they did
Satan certainly would shout.

"Do the taverns close their doors,
Just to take a little rest?
Why, 'twould be the height of nonsense,
For their trade would be distressed;
Did you ever know it happen,
Or hear anybody tell,
Satan takin' a vacation,
Shuttin' up the doors to Hell?

"And shall preachers of the Gospel
Pack their trunks and go away,
Leaving saints and dyin' sinners
To get along as best they may?
Are the souls of saints and sinners
Valued less than selling beer?
Or do preachers tire quicker
Than the rest of mortals here?

"Why it is, I cannot answer,
But my feelings they are stirred;
Here I've dragged my tottering footsteps
For to hear the Gospel word,
But the preacher is a-traveling,
And the meetin' house is closed;
I confess it's very tryin',
Hard, indeed, to keep composed.

"Tell me, when I tread the valley,
And go up the shinin' height,
Will I hear no angels singing?
Will I see no gleaming light?
Will the golden harps be silent?
Will I meet no welcome there?
Why, the thought is most distressin',
Would be more than I could bear.

"Tell me, when I reach the city,
Over on the other shore,
Will I find a little notice,
Tacked upon the golden door,
Telling me, 'mid dreadful silence,
Writ in words that cut and burn,
'Jesus absent on vacation,
Heaven closed till His return'?"

The Atheist

By William Knox

The fool hath said, "There is no God."
No God! Who lights the morning sun,
And sends him on his heavenly road
A far and brilliant course to run?
Who, when the radiant day is done,
Hangs forth the moon's noctournal lamp,
And bids the planets one by one,
Steal o'er the night vales, dark and damp?

No God! Who gives
   the evening dew
The fanning breeze, the
   fostering shower?
Who warms the
   spring morn's
   budding
   bough?
And plants the
   summer's
   noontide
   flower?
Who spreads the
   autumnal bower,
The fruit tree's mellow
   stores around,
And sends the winter's icy power
To invigorate the exhausted ground?

No God! What makes the bird to wing
Its flight like arrow through the sky,
And gives the deer the power to spring

From rock to rock triumphantly?
Who formed Behemoth huge and high
That at a draught the river drains
And great Leviathan to lie,
Like floating isle in ocean plains?

No God! Who warms the heart to heave
With thousand feelings soft and sweet,
   And prompts the aspiring soul to leave
     The earth we tread
       beneath our feet,
        And soar away
         on pinions' feet
         Beyond the scenes
          of mortal strife,
          With fair
           ethereal forms
           to meet
          That tell us of
           the after life?

        No God! Who fixed
         the solid ground
       Of pillars strong,
        that alter not?
      Who spread the curtained skies around?
Who doth the ocean bounds allot?
Who all things to perfection brought
On earth below, in heaven above?
Go ask the fool, of impious thought,
Who dares to say, "There is no God."

Prayer

By George Elliston

I do not always bend the knee to pray.
I often pray in crowded city street,
In some hard crisis of a busy day;
Prayer is my sure and comforting retreat.

"Dear Lord, Thy help," my lips cry silently;
From swiftly moving train my prayer ascends;

My heaven is not afar, but near to me,
And ever from His throne my Father bends.

Here at my office desk I crave His aid;
No matter where I am, I crave His care;
In moments when my soul is most afraid
It comforts most to know He's everywhere.

Only Five Minutes *Author Unknown*

Five minutes late,
And school is begun.
What are rules for,
If you break every one?
Just as the scholars
Are seated and quiet,
You hurry in
With disturbance and riot.

Five minutes late,
And the table is spread.
The children are seated
And grace has been said;
Even the baby,
All sparkling and rosy,
Sits in her chair
By Mamma, so cozy!

Five minutes late,
And your hair all askew,
Just as the comb
Was drawn hastily through;
There is your chair,
And your tumbler and plate,
Cold cheer for those
Who are five minutes late.
Five minutes late

On the bright Sabbath morn,
All the good people
To church they have gone.
Ah, when you stand
At the Beautiful Gate
What will you do
If you're five minutes late?

~~~~~~~~~~~~~~~~~~

Don't Trouble *Author Unknown*

Don't you trouble trouble
Till trouble troubles you.
Don't you look for trouble;
Let trouble look for you.
Who feareth hath forsaken
The heavenly Father's side;
What He hath undertaken
He surely will provide.

The very birds reprove thee
With all their happy song;
The very flowers teach thee
That fretting is a wrong.

"Cheer up," the sparrow chirpeth;
"Thy Father feedeth me;
Think how much He careth,
Oh, lonely child, for thee."

"Fear not," the flowers whisper;
"Since thus He hath arrayed
The buttercup and daisy,
How canst thou be afraid?"
Then don't you trouble trouble
Till trouble troubles you;
You'll only double trouble,
And trouble others, too.

~~~~~~~~~~~~~~~~~~

Life's Book *Author Unknown*

No matter what else you are doing
From cradle days through to the end,
You are writing your life's secret story;
Each day sees another page penned.

Each month ends a thirty-page chapter,
Each year means the end of a part,
And never an act is misstated
Or even one wish of the heart.

Each day when you wake
the book opens
Revealing a page clean and white—
What thoughts and what words
and what doings
Will cover its pages by night?
God leaves that to you—you're the writer
And never a word shall grow dim.
"Finish" and give your life's book to him.

A Woman's Prophecy

*This poem by Mother Shipton was written in the 15th Century.
In it many things that have come to pass are predicted.*

*Mother Shipton was born in 1488 in a cave near Knaresborough, England and died
near York, England in 1561. One of her more famous prophetic poems follows.*

A carriage without horses shall go,
Disaster fill the world with woe;
In London Primrose Hill shall be,
Its center hold a bishop's see.
Around the world men's thoughts shall fly,
Quick as the twinkling of an eye.

And water shall great wonders do—
How strange, and yet it shall come true.
Then upside down the world shall be,
And gold found at the foot of tree;
Though tower hills proud man shall ride,
Nor horse nor ass move by his side.

Beneath the water men shall walk;
Shall ride, shall sleep, and even talk
And in the air men shall be seen,
In white, in black, as well as green.
A great man shall come and go,
For prophecy declares it so.

In water iron then shall float
As easy as a wooden boat.
God shall be found in stream or stone.
In land that is as yet unknown,
Water and fire shall wonder to,
And England shall admit a Jew.

The Jew that once was held in scorn,
Shall of a Christian then be born.
A house of glass shall come to pass
In England—but alas! Alas!
A war will follow with the work
Where dwells the pagan and the Turk.

The states will lock in fierce strife,
And seek to take each other's life;
When North shall thus divide the South,
The eagle builds in lions' mouth.
The tax and blood and cruel war
Shall come to very humble door.

Three times shall sunny, lovely France
Be led to play a bloody dance;
Before the people shall be free
Three tyrant rulers shall she see;
Three rules, in succession, be,
Each sprung from diff'rent dynasty.

Then when the fiercest fight is done,
England and France shall be as one.
The British olive next shall twine
In marriage with the German vine.
Men walk beneath and over streams,
Fulfilled shall be our strangest dreams.

All England's sons shall plow the land.
Shall oft be seen with book in hand.
The poor shall now most wisdom know,
And water wind where corn did grow;
Great houses stand in far-flung vale
And covered o'er with snow and hail.

And now a word in uncouth rhyme,
Of what shall be in future time;
For in those wonderous, far-off days
The women shall adopt a craze
To dress like men and trousers wear,
And cut off their lovely locks of hair.

They'll ride astride with brazen brow
As witches on a broomstick now.
Then love shall die and marriage cease,
And nations wane as babes decrease.
The wives shall fondle cats and dogs,
And men live much the same as hogs.

In nineteen hundred twenty-six
Build houses light of straw and sticks,
For then shall mighty wars be planned,
And fire and sword shall sweep the land,
But those who live the century through,
In fear and trembling this will do.

Flee to the mountains and the dens,
To bog and forests and wild fens—
For storms shall rage and ocean roar
When Gabriel stands on sea and shore;

And as he blows his wondrous horn
Old worlds shall die and new be born.

This is the original Mother Shipton's prophecy.

The Sign of the Cross

Author Unknown

In the camp it is night
And the wind is moaning low.
All is still save the tramp
Of a guard to and fro.

At the outpost, the picket
The weary watch keeps,
Though the clouds
 die and peep
While the universe
 sleeps.

Hark! That sound,
 on the ground,
Someone climbing
 the steep.
Branches break,
 through the slime
They're trying to
 creep.

"Who goes there?"
 rings out
A voice clear and strong.
"It's a friend—weak
From journey long."

"Well, advance friend, advance
And the countersign give.
Otherwise," Sentry cries,
"None this line can pass and live.

"Strict are orders tonight.
I disobey?—I dare not.
For all without the countersign,
On the spot must be shot."

"For God's sake, let me live
 Brave loyal man.
 I've just escaped prison dungeon
 And now, must I die?

"If by friends I'm forgotten,
 Dark and dreary, my lot.
 Weak and weary
 and worn—
 But the password
 I know not.

"I'm a true boy
 in blue,
 But not ready to die
 Send me not
 unprepared
 To that great God
 on high."

"Your sorrow I share,
 But your life
 I cannot spare.
 A brief moment
 I grant you,
 For death to prepare."

 Lo. The wonder there—
 Wrapped in deep vernal prayer,
 He makes the sign of the cross
 With his finger in the air.

"You were saved by God's might!"
He cried in delight,
"For the Sign of the Cross
Was the password tonight."

In My Father's House

Author Unknown

In our sleep we ofttimes wander
In a dreamland bright and fair,
In a land where flowers of beauty
With sweet fragrance scent the air.
There's a dream of golden vision,
Of a heavenly land so bright
That I dreamed of, could I only
Now to you its message write.

Lo, I wandered in a country
Beautiful beyond compare,
Golden harps were ever sounding
Heavenly music in the air.
Rivers, too, as clear as crystals,
Fountains with their silver spray,
And the light of that blest country
Clearer was, than light of day.

As I stood in silent wonder,
One bright form came softly near,
As I looked I knew my Savior,
In His hands the nail prints clear.
Then He touched me on the shoulder
As he spoke in gentle tone:
"In my Father's House are mansions,
Mansions built by love alone.

"Each one here doth claim a mansion."
"Where is mine?" I then replied.
"Come with me," He softly whispered,
And I glided by His side.
How my heart stood still in wonder,
Mansions fair did meet my gaze,
Some they were not yet completed,
Others their stately domes did raise.

And I prayed and I longed so earnest
That I could claim one as mine,
Then a voice, it was my Savior's,
Saying, "This my child is thine."
As I looked I saw a structure
On a grand foundation plan,
Nothing else, no walls, no towers,
Work left off where it began.

"Lord," I cried in anguish sorely,
"Thy unfinished work is mine,"
And his voice was full of sadness
As he spoke those words divine.
"In my Father's House are mansions,
Don't you see and understand,
God is the Great Master builder,
Ye are workers 'neath His hand.

"For by each unselfish action,
And by every gentle word,
Ye are building heavenly mansions
In the city of your God.
Back to earth my child go calmly
And thy work take up with zeal,
Lay thy treasures in this kingdom
Where no thieves break through nor steal."

"Lord," I cried in anguish sorely,
"I was blind, I did not care,
'Twas the things of earth I cherished
Not my heavenly mansion fair,
But my life is in Thy keeping,
All I have, and am is Thine,
Lead, O lead me in Thy footsteps,
To that heavenly life divine."

'Twas a dream but there's a message,
Meant for all this world to know.
Just pass on a word of kindness,
In life's pathway here below;
Bear ye one another's burdens,
As ye walk along the road;
Those the stones that build your mansion
In the heavenly home of God.

Just to help on life's short journey,
Some poor soul along the way,
Just to take their hand in kindness,
And a gentle word to say,
What is wealth or what is pleasure?
We shall leave those all behind;
When we cross the heavenly portal,
We immortal joys shall find.

The Land of Beulah

Author Unknown

I am dwelling on the mountain
Where the golden sunlight beams;
O'er a land where wondrous beauty
Far exceeds my fondest dreams.
Where the air is pure, ethereal,
Laden with the breath of flowers,
They are blooming by the fountain
'Neath the amaranthine bowers.

Refrain:
Is not this the land of Beulah?
Blessed, blessed land of light;
Where the flowers bloom forever
And the sun is always bright.

I can see far down the mountain
Where I wandered weary years,
Often hindered in my journey
By the ghosts of doubts and fears.
Broken vows and disappointments
Thickly sprinkled all the way,
But the Spirit led, unerring,
To the land I hold today.

I am drinking at the fountain
Where I ever would abide;
For I've tasted life's pure river
And my soul is satisfied.
There's no thirsting for life's pleasures,
Nor adorning, rich and gay,
For I've found a richer treasure,
One that fadeth not away.

Title Index

Author Index

First Line Index

Last Line Index